Automatic Self-Discipline: Unlock the Power of the Subconscious Mind

Learn the Secret Techniques to Train Your Brain to Never Procrastinate, Directly Pursue Goals, and Develop Habits Without Distraction. The Ultimate Beginner's Guide.

Leo Black

Table of Contents

Introduction

Benjamin Franklin once said: "You may delay, but time will not." Procrastination comes in all shapes and sizes, at any given moment, and happens to anyone. You probably find yourself standing in front of a brick wall more often than you like to admit. You're unsure of where it started, but you know that your life has taken a turn thanks to this delaying tactic inside of you. I too found myself in this position, sitting at the table wondering what happened and how to fix it. Putting things off can seem so insignificant at first until we can't ignore it anymore.

"I have so much time left."

"I can start this project tomorrow because I don't feel up to it today."

"What difference will one day make in paying my rent?"

"My car's check engine light is flashing but I know it can go another 500 miles before I attend to it."

"My wife doesn't need to know about me losing my job until I have another one."

"I can defy my boss because I am untouchable and irreplaceable."

"I work better when I cram everything into the last hour."

Do any of these statements ring a bell with you? You might be the person who pushed your car until it broke down on the way to work. The consequences started snowballing: you delayed the repairs and had to spend money you didn't have to spare. These costs would never have been there if you allowed the warning light to penetrate your subconscious cycle. You arrive late at work and lo and behold, you never finished the presentation either. You planned to finish at the office just before you were supposed to deliver it.

The fact that you're paid for delivered work also didn't bother you until now. You're not sure if you crave the adrenalin that comes from a last-minute push, or maybe you just hate taking orders from your boss? You know that he pays your salary when you deliver, but why must he dictate your schedule if you're in control of how much work you earn money from? You've never been friends with deadlines before and start feeling a panic seep into your mind. You know how many times you've let your boss down and wonder how long it will be before he fires you.

Your worst fears come true as you're called into his office and dismissed. What the heck do you do now? Your head starts spinning and you don't know what your next move is. You're not good at planning anything or following through. You have to keep this a secret from your husband or wife until you find another job. That's the only thing that springs to mind when suddenly, your phone rings. It's your landlord and you remember that your rent is late as your work was delayed. Besides, you handed your last savings over to the tow company this morning.

Finally, it dawns on you that you've lost control of everything. You can't postpone telling your spouse about your unemployment and you can't avoid your landlord either. You have an epiphany while standing at the lake. You are a procrastinator, and your prolonged behavior has led to consequences that crushed you under a mountain of stress and uncertainty.

This is one example of what can happen in a procrastinator's life. It's also an extreme example where the person has been delaying things for a long time. You have no option left other than facing the enemy called procrastination.

Chances are that the procrastinator's habit started in school when they continued to study at the last minute to skid through an exam. Eventually, their workplace became a mess and so did their home and romantic lives. Many delayers become depressed, anxious, exhausted, stressed, and overwhelmed when things take a turn for the worst. Some of us will lose our jobs while others may end up losing their homes, livelihoods, status, reputation, reliability, friends, family, and even opportunities. Procrastination comes with mild to severe consequences and the only way we can defeat this nemesis is by learning how to be productive.

Many procrastinators have tried and tested numerous methods, failing time and again. They couldn't understand why they procrastinate. Some people learn why but they still succumb to internal consequences. The guilt, shame, and humiliation can be overpowering. Procrastinators lose the hope and self-empowerment required to become productive people again. They think this behavior is out of their control because they don't understand it. The truth is that procrastinators who are forcefully made aware of their behavior through consequences are prepared and willing to change their ways. Often, they can feel alone in this procrastination role and turn to other procrastination methods that are more harmful than good.

If you're one of the delayers who think you're alone, think again. Twenty-six percent of Americans are chronic procrastinators nowadays, versus there only being five percent in 1978 (Gaille, 2017). Students are the most affected with figures between 85% and 95%, which indicates further progression into the next generation. Look at the bright side of things; you aren't in the worst generation right now. Also, 20% of Americans procrastinate so much that they risk their credit ratings, jobs, homes, health, and relationships. Over 40% of these delayers have already suffered financial consequences.

It gets worse as we learn that 95% of Americans procrastinate mildly and occasionally during their lives.

Fifty-seven percent of students explained that they enjoy the rush that comes from putting assignments off until the last minute. To break this down further, let's see how this habit affects our happiness levels: 46% of delayers believe that procrastination impacts their lives moderately, whereas 18% of them express deep displeasure and severe consequences from it.

Those who admitted to the extreme negativities have shared their worst consequences. Extreme anxiety, clinical depression, obsessive-compulsive tendencies, attention challenges, and failed memory were among the top internal consequences listed in this statistical briefing. Procrastinators who admit to their habits have explained that this becomes their lifestyle. So, you're not alone in this. Moving from awareness to forming new habits is motivated by your desire among other factors.

This book is about overcoming the habit of procrastination. I've been there and done that. I've stood where you are right now. The best way to move you forward is to focus only on the necessary theory and quickly dive into the practical steps you'll need.

- Overcoming procrastination in your life is achievable even if you've already tried reading 10 books about it. Many of them contain wonderful insight into what happens in our brains when we delay tasks, however, they don't give us practical and reliable exercises we can implement in seconds to overcome our procrastination habit. You'll learn to train your brain and subconscious mind rather than only learning about what's wrong with it.

You'll have answers to these questions and more when you're done with this book:

- Why do I procrastinate so much?
- Am I just being lazy or is this a deeper issue?
- Which type am I and what consequences can come from it?
- How does my brain control me when I postpone important things?
- What have I been doing wrong until now?
- What are the most common justifications used?
- How does my brain form these habits and can I change them?
- Are there simple and fast-acting exercises to halt the process of procrastination?
- Where do I start when I have a problem with starting things?
- Can I stop all the distractions that tempt me to stray?
- How fast do these changes happen?
- Am I a lost cause after trying everything under the sun already?
- Are goals just a fallacy or have I been doing it wrong?

- What's the right way of accomplishing happiness and deserved pride?
- Can I learn about the secret technique that stops procrastination in minutes?

The techniques in this book are simple, practical, and motivational to help you follow through with them. You won't only adjust your behavior, you'll also learn to optimize it for maximum benefits. I'll even introduce you to the well-known myth you probably tried that led to failure. The reason for that failure will be revealed too. Much of the advice we get from social groups and online sources are fraught with this mythical technique that is psychologically counterproductive.

This is where you make a decision that could change your life. Continue reading if you'd like to find solutions and remove the risk of severe consequences from your life.

Part 1:

Understanding…

Procrastination is like a sly fox that must be exposed for what it is. You have to learn about the basics and understand how it sneaks up on you. You've reached the first milestone of awareness by admitting that you might have a problem with delay tactics. Now we can delve into further details to make sure you aren't overlooking other snippets you're prone to. Part one of this informative guide will help you understand everything you need to know and no more than that. There are various types of procrastinators, an ocean of potential consequences, and a cycle of resistance that happens automatically. This section will teach you about the brain and how sponge-like it is as well.

Chapter 1:

Procrastination: Your Worst Enemy

Procrastination can be the thorn in our side if we are unable to identify and eradicate it. The problem is that many people don't understand what procrastination truly is. Even worse, they don't know how many types of procrastinators there are out there. They have this idea that a procrastinator is defined as someone who doesn't get anything done or always misses their deadlines at work. Some people see this problem in those who use the hair-raising term "tomorrow is another day." While these are all correct definitions, there are a few more that slip under the radar. We also need to understand what the consequences of "putting things off for a better day" are and what they can do to us. We'll open your understanding of these key elements of procrastination while teaching you why it's not entirely bad in some cases.

A Comprehensive Look

What is procrastination in comprehensible terms? If we look at the Latin origins of the word, we see that 'pro' translates to forward, and 'crastinate' means tomorrow. It's seemingly straightforward, but people still don't fully understand what this word can widely include. For example, it can be used to describe someone who chooses to carry out less relevant tasks instead of dealing with more pressing issues. It also describes someone who prefers more pleasurable options to the less enjoyable choice. Procrastinators also postpone these tasks until a later time or date, and in some cases, can even leave the task until the last minute. Keep in mind that we're using the word 'task' to simplify things for now, but it can also be an assignment, workplace deadline, social interaction, experience, activity, or general responsibility towards oneself or another person.

A less common type of procrastinator is someone who rushes through their day, putting off one task for another, and has no structure to their day. There's no planning involved and this person can't even tell you what they're doing for lunch. Unplanned days and erratic "last minute" changes are a sure description of someone delaying the inevitable. Many people turn this type of procrastinating into an art form of unpredictability and surprise. The worst part is that these people don't always acknowledge their persistent delays and turn the day into a free-for-all. Nothing is planned and they have no direction. The entire day is about winging the next task. It's even hard for other people to see this behavior in them because their friends think they're spontaneous, impulsive, and adventurous. There's no doubt that these people might experience something amazing during their freefall, but it's a high risk, low reward behavior.

The truth is that procrastination can be prevalent in our home lives, relationships, careers, academia, and even our self-care rituals. Stressful and less enjoyable activities are simply part of life. One of the largest instigators for delay tactics is that we allow our fears, emotions, and a deep desire for pleasure to provoke this issue further. It's a subconscious process that happens below the level of our consciously-aware thoughts. That's why it can happen in any part of our lives. Procrastination has been studied vastly. Academic delay tactics have been one of the largest concerns. Psychologist Gregory Schraw and his associates researched academic students to understand what the true definition of procrastination was (Schraw et al., 2007).

The irrefutable new definition describes someone who intentionally delays an intended course of action, even if they'll be in a worse situation for doing so. However, Schraw and his colleagues also confirm those delay tactics are a behavioral issue. The way we can determine whether we are procrastinators or not is to identify whether we have the three common factors related to it. The three cornerstones are counterproductivity, needlessness, and persistent delay. Is the choice you've made counterproductive to your result? You must decide whether you're better off for doing it now or delaying a task for a later time or date. Workplace delays are simple to distinguish for counterproductivity. Delaying a task will require anxious pressure to finish it before the deadline. Not everyone can work under pressure and so this is counterproductive.

Needlessness is another simple aspect of it. You can determine how commonly you use this by asking yourself whether your delay was necessary. Someone who delayed their work due to rushing to their child's school for an emergency cannot relate to needlessness. However, someone who delays their responsibility because they stumbled upon an online sale certainly shows a needless aspect.

The third piece of the procrastination puzzle is self-explanatory. Delay tactics wouldn't be defined as such unless you delayed your activity for one that was more enjoyable or less important. Filtering any actions through these three cornerstones can help you identify whether you're procrastinating or being too hard on yourself.

Indeed, some delays can't be classified as procrastination. This means that we must also define what isn't considered procrastination or we won't fully understand it. Clarity is divided by what we call active and passive procrastination. Passive procrastinators would tick all three cornerstone boxes we mentioned. Active procrastinators are those who are more productive and content with their delay tactics. One differentiating condition is to say that passive procrastinators are the kind of people who delay actions because they don't have the skills necessary, the confidence in themselves, or simply don't or can't act in time. They usually find that the results aren't in their best interests.

Active procrastinators either have a reason for delaying the task or love working under pressure. These types of people still complete their work on time and might even achieve great results. Psychologist Jin Nam Choi from Seoul National University and Angela Hsin Chun Chu from Columbia University studied the differences between 230 active and passive procrastinating undergraduates at three Canadian universities (Novotney, 2010). The active and passive students were spending similar amounts of time procrastinating. The results showed that the active procrastinators were still showing productive usage of their time, good academic performance, and even built an adaptive skill to procrastination itself.

Realistically, it isn't active procrastination if you aren't satisfied with the outcome, don't have a preference for working under pressure, aren't intentionally doing it, or you're missing deadlines. Deadlines aren't necessarily work-related as mentioned before. A deadline could be an important conversation you were supposed to have.

Let's say that Joe invited his girlfriend Susan to go sky-diving and she's terrified of heights. Susan will have an internal deadline for when she needs to tell Joe. The outcome will be devastating and Susan doesn't like the pressure this deadline adds to her romantic life. She also isn't intentionally delaying the conversation, but she's afraid of letting Joe down.

She has missed the deadline to chat about this as soon as the plane left the ground. This gives us an example of a passive procrastinator. If we look at the other side of the coin, we realize that Susan might've waited strategically for a later date to mention her fear of heights. She didn't see the conversation as relevant at the time because Joe was revealing the upcoming adventure trip in front of his entire family. It wasn't the right time to discuss it because he was too excited.

This gives you an idea of active versus passive. There are also four considerations for active procrastination. These could be beneficial under certain circumstances.

Relevance: The first type of active delay can be seen in people who deliberately choose to delay an irrelevant task based on their preferences. The truth is that an activity might be relevant to someone else and not to you. This includes the sky-diving incident. It could also include a task at work which doesn't interest you and you'd do better with another task. It's a question of relevancy to your passions, ambitions, and preferences. It can also mean that you place more emphasis on tasks that need attention faster. For example, postponing a shopping trip for your mom is acceptable when you prioritize your assignment that's due tomorrow. Groceries are relevant to your mom, but your assignment is more urgent and relevant to your long-term success.

Consequences: The next factor for active procrastination is weighing the consequences against delaying the activity. Active delayers can measure the consequences as either good, acceptable, or over the top before they intentionally delay a task. This helps them make smart and productive choices. This can certainly help people who need to bridge the gap between reason and intuition. Allowing themselves some time for pondering the details will help them identify a decision that could be productive or counterproductive. Our intuitions aren't always correct and sometimes we can rush into an activity without giving it realistic contemplation.

Strategic delays: Sometimes, we need a strategic delay because our minds aren't quite ready yet. We might not know what's needed or our understanding might be minimal. Active procrastinators will use this intentional delay to give themselves time to learn more about what they must do. One thing we don't realize is that our minds are subconsciously on the task even when we're busy with something else. It will continually gather data and think about the best result before we dive into the activity itself. People are often amazed at themselves for having more answers when the deadline draws closer and they finally jump into the project.

Self-expectation: The next benefit of active procrastination is when we finally recognize that we're being way too hard on ourselves. Our expectations are unrealistic and that's why we fear the start of a task. Active procrastinators give themselves time to understand and accept their expectations for what they are. This can help us adjust our expectations to accurate levels. Remember that active procrastinators develop an adaptive state of mind and this is how they adjust those expectations. You'd need to readjust your expectations again if you're still meeting deadlines but continue to procrastinate endlessly. This means that you're an active procrastinator who benefits from these planned delays, so stop being hard on yourself.

Now you have a great understanding of what defines procrastination, both active and passive. This will help you identify which type of procrastinator you are because delaying tasks for certain reasons can be to your advantage rather than a dreaded behavior. There needs to be a balance though. Active procrastinators aren't the type who lounge on the couch all day.

Procrastinator Types

There are numerous types of procrastinators among us and we can identify certain behavioral traits to distinguish which kinds we might be. There are six main types of delayers: knowing which one we are can help us devise a proper strategy for overcoming the problem. Keep in mind that all six categories can be active or passive procrastinators.

The perfectionist: The first one on our list is closely related to someone who has high expectations of themselves. The only difference between active and passive delayers here will be whether they can adapt or not. Perfectionists have irrational expectations of themselves and their greatest ambition is to be the best at what they do. It doesn't matter if they're contemplating relationships, work, home, or personal care. They become stricken with fear of not being perfect in their results and, therefore, they dawdle away. They give up on themselves because they cannot fathom the idea of not obtaining perfect scores. This is a common problem for many of us.

The dreamer: This is the type of person who delays tasks because they can't focus on them. Daydreaming, fantasizing, and having no control over their attention is the main cause of concern here. These people will struggle to pay attention to detail as soon as something seems complex or boring to them. This includes someone who chooses not to start their task because there's something more interesting on their minds. They might be looking forward to a weekend getaway and can't stop their mind from focusing on this. It's hard to wrap up a report at work when all you can think of is your feet sinking into the hot sand on the beach tomorrow.

The defier: The defiant delayer is as stubborn as they come. They don't like other people telling them what to do or giving them restraints of any kind. This becomes unusually problematic with time schedules as defiers can refuse to be dictated to by someone giving them a deadline. This includes their employers and romantic partners and can be highly detrimental. The defier is often complacent in their opinions and doesn't like other people giving them advice or restrictions, therefore, they'd rather delay the task because it's not that important to them. Timelines aren't a priority if it comes from another person's mouth, especially someone superior at work.

The worrier: This type of procrastinator is someone who suffers from an unusual balance of having no confidence and the fear of change. Everyone has a hint of fear inside of them, but it's dangerous when this fear starts affecting your potential. The worrier will procrastinate because their boss gave them a new responsibility at work and they're afraid of stepping out of their comfort zones. They can be quite confident in the responsibilities they are familiar with, but fear strikes as soon as they take on something new. We can see this type in our personal lives too: for example, a man might fear moving in with his girlfriend because it's all so new to them. New environments and tasks strike fear in this kind of delayers.

The crisis-maker: Some people will rather put tasks off for a later date because they love the rush and adrenaline that come from the urgency. It's strange to think that some people love working under pressure, but think about standard job applications: they always ask whether you're capable of working under pressure. We all tick that box but truthfully, we don't all thrive in pressurized environments, even when employers try to make it look like a normal thing. Crisis-managers are great as long as they are meeting their deadlines, but it's damaging when they're passive procrastinators. We'll all face times where pressure is prevalent in the workplace and home, but someone who seeks this rush with intentional delay is a crisis-maker.

The overdoer: This person is the final type of procrastinator that can also be mistaken for a perfectionist. The overdoer is someone who takes on more than they can handle realistically. One can say that they have too much confidence in their ability to get everything done and end up burning the candle at both ends. Human beings are only capable of so much and when they take on more than what is reasonably acceptable, their minds will switch the delay tactics on. Suddenly, they realize that they're overwhelmed and struggle to find time to start and complete their tasks. The sheer thoughts of their overestimation on their logical skills and abilities are brought to light and they delay their task while trying to find a solution. Unfortunately, passive procrastinators often also overlook solutions.

The human psyche is capable of more than some people believe, and less than others think. Identifying your major and sub-types of procrastination will be the first step in finding that fine line between more and less.

The Consequences

A huge part of knowing our enemy is to understand what the consequences of procrastination are. This can help us realize what needs to be done about it and find ways of avoiding repetition. It can also help us recognize whether we're suffering from behavioral procrastination or not. There are numerous internal and external consequences of this behavior that we don't deserve or need in our lives. The truth is that chronic procrastination can affect your psyche and become an adopted lifestyle rather than a time-management crisis. The consequences can seep into our professional, personal, financial, and social lives before we know it.

You could damage your relationships with friends, family, romantic partners, and even your colleagues. Delay tactics are seen as a failure to make decisions by your social crowd and resentment can grow. Let's go back to the couple from the sky-diving incident here. Susan has broken Joe's trust if she withheld her fears for no reason. Being open and honest with your social group is necessary to maintain healthy relationships. Susan's fear of sharing something as intimate as anxiety driven by an earth-shattering fear doesn't strengthen the relationship. It hurts Joe and builds resentment between them.

This could lead to the relationship ending in extreme cases and this will only hurt Susan emotionally. Also, her additional fears will be amplified in the future because she's already failed at a relationship. Now she's convinced that future relationships will fail as well. Insecurities and loneliness can be a consequence in your relationships if the delay tactics have been severe enough to end the bond. The same applies to your job. The consequences of broken trust can lead to many issues along the line. Most people we work with and those in our social circles see our word as a promise. They expect us to follow through with something when we say we will. Delaying a presentation at work when your boss is depending on you can harm your reputation.

The longer this takes place, the more your reputation will become tarnished with colleagues and friends. The trust that was once placed in your empty promises has been broken. Trust is an insanely difficult thing to get back once it's gone. These are mainly external damages, but the internal damage comes when no one relies on you anymore and your self-esteem is trampled into submission. Low self-esteem will only worsen the procrastination problem because you won't have faith in yourself anymore. You could become anxious or depressed when people leave your life or you feel like you can't do anything right anymore.

Stress is a silent killer and chronic procrastination will increase it no matter how you think you can avoid it. Leaving everything for the last minute or persistently disappointing yourself and others will elevate your stress levels subconsciously and biologically. Stress can place your overall health at risk too. It leads to a chemical imbalance in your brain that could eventually impact your heart, blood pressure, and even cause weight fluctuations. Chronic procrastination can also impact your health when you keep postponing your exercise routines and self-care. These factors will inflate your fears and could also come back to bite you in the backside when you start making poor decisions because you're insecure.

Now you can shift from one type of delayer to another. Suddenly, you can become an overthinker which causes you to find reasons for delaying projects based on facts that weren't there to begin with. The worst is that all of these consequences are intertwined with each other and start snowballing into an avalanche of dramatic significance. Your hurt reputation could lead to you losing your job. The internal consequences of losing your financial stability funnel straight into shame and self-blame, knocking your self-esteem even lower. The damage to your personal relationships can also snowball into depression and eventually accidents or physical injury. It's an infinite cycle of self-defeating outcomes on a subconscious level.

It might start small when you lose time and have to make it up, but it also leads to missed opportunities and self-derogatory notions. Every aspect of procrastination has internal and external consequences. To put it in simple terms, relationships can be lost, careers can be destroyed, and financial ruin can knock on your door. You could also place your health at grave risk and miss out on accomplishments that should've been yours to take. You can start missing goals that will set you back further when you disappoint yourself. Your self-esteem will decrease more and you'll put in even less effort, leading to a poor reputation at work or home.

Some procrastinators can even become unintentional delinquents when they end up not paying their taxes and bills on time, leaving them with rebates, stressful relocations, and humiliation.

Humiliation is a strong emotion that can come from many of these consequences. For example, Sarah keeps missing her bill payments and hasn't filed her taxes this year. She stands a chance of painful audits and losing her home. She could even go to jail for tax evasion. These are the external consequences, whereas the internal consequences are vast. She feels depressed, anxious, stressed out, humiliated, stupid, and incapable to mention a few.

Let's say that John has delayed his conversation with Lily as a less extreme example. John hasn't been happy in his relationship for weeks and has continued to delay the inevitable in the hopes of Lily breaking things off with him first. John's external consequences happen when his family and friends resent him and start avoiding him because he complains about Lily every day, without doing something about it. John also wrestles with mixed emotions, some of which are detrimental to his wellbeing because he forces himself to stay in a relationship that makes him miserable: that's his internal consequence.

Consequences and their awareness help us understand the final factor in identifying our procrastination so that we can move onto the next part of removing it from our lives.

Chapter 2:

Round and Round: Here We Go Again

Procrastination is a psychological and biological process that happens in cycles. Just as many things in life are relative, so is procrastination. We're going to introduce you to delay tactics that take place in cycles that can extend over days, weeks, months, or even years. There are emotions and thoughts attached to these points that have become so automatic that you hardly notice them anymore. Procrastination isn't just a behavior. Behavior is instigated by thoughts that open you up to emotions. We'll discuss the psychological process soon enough, but for now, we want you to recognize where you are on this timeline. Awareness is an essential step in understanding your cycle because everyone's sequence is different.

The Loop Starts

Our cycle often starts with a promise we make to ourselves. Keep in mind that this often begins after you've already had an encounter with procrastination. You might've missed a deadline at work, or you might be like John who failed to end a relationship until he was so miserable that even his friends and family avoided him. The word cycle refers to a loop, much like a circle that has no start and no end. However, this loop forms before you know it and you find yourself stuck in a cycle of endless delays. You might even go for a few weeks or months without noticing any delay tactics. We'll emphasize that the cycle is varied from person to person. Yours might be an annual thing, but it could also complete the roundabout every couple of weeks. A smaller, shorter cycle can be worrisome as you may have come to a point where procrastination isn't healthy anymore.

Nevertheless, the true origin of the circle is as soon as you promise yourself that you'll do things differently this time. The most common promise is: "I'll start early this time." Other common promises include: "I can do this with time to spare" and "I won't let things get out of hand this time." This is where it starts and this behavior can often be associated with self-trust. You trust yourself and that's where the thoughts come in. The problem is that procrastinators don't keep this promise, even if it's an assurance to themselves. Delayers also don't intend on lying to themselves like this, but they hardly ever keep this promise. They realize the truth before they know it though. The next part of the cycle is usually echoed in the words: "I have to start soon." We know that this statement is true, but things are more complicated than just knowing it.

John wants to break up with his girlfriend, so he has to do something soon even if he goes through the entire cycle. He knows that he will only become more miserable and his relationship won't miraculously change course overnight. Lily won't suddenly turn into the woman of his dreams.

John could be the same at work, as some procrastinators use their delay tactics in multiple areas of their lives. He might have a presentation at work next week and has started his cycle with the empty promise which was followed by the reality of needing to start. He needs to start soon because his boss is relying on him to pull out all the stops. Besides, his boss gave him more than enough time to complete the presentation. All he has to do is start working.

The next part of the cycle is often expressed in a question. "What if I don't start my presentation?" "What if I don't break up with Lily?" This part of the cycle begins unraveling the thoughts and emotions tied to procrastination. It's possibly the first part of the circle that awakens our fears. It can also be where we realize that time has slipped away from us. We are terrible at managing our time and it will show, no matter how we try to deny it. The thoughts that come with the third part of the cycle include: "I should've started sooner," "I can't enjoy anything," or "I hope no one finds out." You could also start misusing the word 'but' when you think that you're doing everything but nothing's happening. Most of these thoughts are easy to understand.

You know that you should've started sooner. This is a normal thought that crosses your mind when reality first strikes. Not enjoying anything is a self-defeating thought. This could happen to people who don't do well with working under pressure. It can be accompanied by self-blame, guilt, and shame. These people start thinking that their lives revolve around negative experiences. However, if we gave ourselves more time to complete a task, we wouldn't have these thoughts. Hoping that no one finds out is another negative thought because this person is feeling guilty. They know they've placed the presentation and the new client at risk by postponing the work. They hope that no one finds out because this could be detrimental to their job.

The final part of the third cycle step revolves around the word 'but.' That word is a passive voice in your inner dialogue. John thinks he's doing everything *but* Lily still sticks around. He has been a complete douche *but* she won't break it off. He isn't actively taking charge of the situation because he passively expects her to break it off.

The Curve

The curve at the bottom of the circle is a dangerous one. It starts with another promise procrastinators make to themselves. "There's still time" is an example of a mindset we enter before the loop reaches its upward turn. We understand this as a phase of denial. Our mind will send us into a declining state of denial to protect itself from reality. John thinks there's still time. Yes, his boss has given him a week to design the perfect presentation, but he has done it last minute before and succeeded. His inner dialogue is sticking to the passive voice by using the word 'but' again. He is bartering mentally and might even convince himself that there's enough time remaining. Let's take the sky-diving incident here. Susan is bartering time because she thinks it's in her control.

She thinks there's enough time left to tell Joe that she's terrified of heights before they jump out of an airplane tomorrow. Susan momentarily forgets that the longer she waits to tell Joe, the more awkward the conversation will be. John has the same predicament with Lily. He keeps thinking that there's more time and he'll break it off with her before it gets worse. All of these can be productive thoughts if you end the loop here, but most passive procrastinators can't. This is only the bottom curve of the circle. The curve is about to lead to an uphill battle. Think about the stress already brewing at this stage. To top this off, a procrastinator could hit the uphill struggle with little to no enthusiasm.

The fifth step of the loop is when we try to convince ourselves of a damaging statement; "there's something wrong with me." Now we start questioning our abilities, skills, time management, previous decisions, self-esteem, and evitable procrastination. Much of the loop has been below our awareness until we start on the incline towards the end of the circle. Procrastinators can feel overwhelmed at this stage as they feel like they've let themselves and others down. "I know that something's wrong with me because I can never complete something I start" or "Something's wrong with me because I can't put my happiness first and break up with the person who makes me miserable", or even "Something is wrong with me because I have no time management skills."

Acknowledgment and guilt can swarm you at the bottom curve. Your stress levels will also shoot through the roof as you realize that something needs to change. You'll have to have that awkward conversation or work through the night to make sure your presentation isn't below par.

The Peak

The sixth step of the loop is when you come to the crossroads and you need to decide how you'll reach the peak again. There are two options procrastinators can take here. The question is to do or not to do because each will take you down another path.

John might use the "to do" approach with his work and the "not to do" angle with his girlfriend. Procrastinators don't always have the same cycles across the board. Remember that every person and every situation is unique: you probably will experience most of the steps, if not all of them, but the crossroads is where the defining decision comes. The choice of not doing the task is where procrastinators risk everything. Thoughts that accompany this can include "I can't stand this" and "why bother?" Both of these thoughts happen when someone gives up on themselves and the task at hand.

John falls into the "why bother" mode at work and could lose his job. He might not notice the persistent cycles but maybe his boss has noticed that he frequently misses deadlines. The clients arrive and John has no presentation ready or he has thrown something together last minute. He made no efforts because he doesn't think he needs to bother with it. Unfortunately, this is a dangerous thought and people always need to bother with their exams, presentations, and even personal aspirations to be content in the end. People who choose this path will either not do the work or half-ass the job.

Someone who thinks they can't stand this anymore is also falling into deep waters. John cannot stand the fact that he's miserable with Lily and quits trying. He throws his hands in the air and goes with the flow. He accepts his fate with her and this is damaging because it can go on for weeks, months, or years before he changes course. Keep in mind that John will reach a peak at some point. The path he chooses on the crossroads will determine how long he must continue his suffering before he gets there. The other crossroad comes with a few options too. The "to do" path ignites an urge to not wait any longer. One can call this an epiphany of sorts. John wakes up subconsciously and realizes that he must do something or he won't progress on the incline. He cannot wait any longer and must break things off with Lily. He can't wait any longer and must work overnight to get his presentation done on time. This is where some procrastinators thrive on the adrenalin they're addicted to. It can go well or it can go terribly wrong.

John could put together a smashing presentation or he could squeeze himself for time and hurt the quality of it. We must realize that active procrastinators are capable of working under pressure and succeeding; however, there is no guarantee that they will. Regularly overworking yourself can lead to burnout.

John could also reach this epiphany with Lily and things could go one of two ways. He can either break things off unexpectedly and finally be free of the bad relationship. He might reach this stage at an inconvenient time and have a complete outburst, breaking things off harshly and hurting himself and Lily in the process.

Timing is everything when it comes to the circle, but the way we handle our timeous steps also matters.

John could be skating on thin ice by completing the loop frequently at work, eventually succumbing to the wrong path at the crossroads. On the other hand, his loop with Lily was prolonged to a point where he will now enter the same dangerous waters with future relationships. But fear not, there are two other options to the "to do" path. John could realize that this isn't so bad and ask himself why he didn't start his presentation sooner. He dives into the work and recognizes how easy it is, or how much he enjoys it. He could also realize this with Lily and ask himself why he didn't break things off sooner. Now he has a broad smile that reflects his inner thoughts of how this isn't so bad. Heck, Lily might even confirm that she was also thinking about breaking things off.

The third option for the "to do" path is as simple as realizing that he just needs to get things done. Suddenly, the "to do" path can boost his incline dramatically, making him confident in his abilities again.

That brings us to the peak of the circle. Let's take a revised look at the loop before learning about the peak.

Step One: You promise yourself that you'll start early this time.

Step Two: You acknowledge the truth that you need to start soon.

Step Three: You ask yourself what would happen if you don't start. Thoughts that accompany this step include:

"I've done everything but it isn't working."

"I'm incapable of enjoying things."

"Why the heck didn't I start sooner?"

"I hope people don't find out about my nonchalant attitude."

Step Four: The fallacy of "there's still time" crosses your mind.

Step Five: Self-doubt creeps in and you think something's wrong with you.

Step Six: The crossroads come in the form of to do or not to do.

The "not to do" path includes thoughts like "why bother?" or "I can't stand this."

The "to do" path includes "let's do this," "I cannot wait any longer," and "this isn't as bad as I feared so why didn't I start sooner?"

Step Seven: This is the peak of your circle and seals the fate of the next cycle if procrastination continues. The moment you loop back over the top curve, you make yourself another promise. Saying: "I'll never procrastinate again" is as common as breathing at this point. We've just completed a circle that taught us a lesson, either good or bad. It might've come with consequences or it might've opened our eyes. Regardless, we'll always convince ourselves that we won't do it again. However, this promise circles back into the first step again.

Chapter 3:

Your Mind is a Curious Organ

Now we can delve into the psychological process of procrastination. We understand what happens, the different types, and what the consequences can be. We also learned about the endless cycle, much like a circle that has no end and no beginning. However, this doesn't make much sense until you understand how the circle officially starts. Where are the origins of your delay tactics? We need to understand the psychological aspect of it before you can see where it began. This chapter will focus on the roots, how procrastination actually works, and some of the most common justifications that we conjure up. We cannot defeat an enemy unless we know how it functions.

The Mechanisms

There are two mechanisms in which procrastination functions, according to psychologist Willem Knaus (Knaus, 2002). This is the subconscious process I've mentioned before. Knaus understood that procrastination could be a pure form of intentional avoidance for some people, but what others don't realize is that their brains go through these mechanisms. The first process is referred to as an "impulse to delay." Impulsiveness is a huge factor in procrastination. It means that we make decisions based on irrational emotions or fears. It can also mean that we strongly, but suddenly, think that delaying a task will lead to a better result. There are so many excuses that come with this process, both good and bad.

I impulsively choose to start a project for school tomorrow because my brain feels foggy today. I think that I'll concentrate better tomorrow. We might feel stressed out today, or we can feel sad because something happened. Let's use John here as an example again. John impulsively delays his breakup with Lily because he is enjoying her humorous company today. They're among friends and it doesn't seem right to do it now. He thinks that tomorrow will be a better day for it because he can be more effective then. Meanwhile, his boss is still relying on him to give that presentation, but he's having too much fun today and would miss out if he focused on the project instead of enjoying time with his friends.

An impulse to delay is often triggered by fears, negative moods, discomforts, threats, anticipated dullness, and perceived negative conditions. John believes that the conditions aren't right to break it off with Lily today. He also believes that his mood will impact the quality of his work on the presentation today. In another example, a student might see their assignment as a tedious bore waiting to happen. So, they put it off as long as they can. Someone else might delay an experience due to perceived threats, such as Susan from the earlier example, who is afraid of heights. This isn't the only threat in her mind, because she also fears losing her boyfriend as a consequence of letting him down. Fear is an assured instigator for procrastination. Many passive procrastinators are slaves to their fears because they have no impulse control.

The second mechanism is when you reassure yourself that starting tomorrow is the right choice. This process is irrefutably intertwined with the first mechanism. Moods, fears, and irrational thoughts are powerful influencers in your mind, especially if you aren't aware of them. Your subconscious mind moves all of these fears forward and you start making conscious excuses and decisions. The subconscious mind is capable of controlling your conscious mind if you don't keep your reins tight.

Nevertheless, the second process is recognized in the excuses you make to confirm the validity of your delay. You might tell yourself that you need time to warm up, feel a certain way, or give the task more thought. You underestimate your abilities and rather give in to the fears that loom. You might also simply have an absurd concept of time. Trust me, this is more common than you believe. We constantly underestimate how much time we need to complete a task. We then overestimate how much time remains. These two mechanisms can be both active or passive as well. The person who outright takes a nap or fiddles with their friend's work instead of their own is actively avoiding their task.

The person who spends more time making excuses is turning the process into a passive act. The passive person is the one who says that tomorrow is another day. Unfortunately, both active and passive delayers often spend more mental energy on avoiding the task than they would've spent on the project itself. These mechanisms also become vastly complicated when passive delayers start justifying their actions with seemingly rational and unchangeable excuses. "Mistakes were made" is one of the most common excuses. "Time was not on my side" is another concoction of disaster.

Active procrastinators also overcomplicate their mechanisms. They avoid the justification stage by ignoring the task altogether. Saying "I'm going to sleep now" when you have a pressing task can only be poor planning. This person doesn't even bother justifying their sudden nap.

The Roots

There are two main roots of procrastination behavior. One has already been explained to some extent. Emotional avoidance is a human flaw that many of us live with. Our emotions can drive our responses in any situation. We delay the tasks we fear; we also delay tasks when we feel emotionally unwell. Perfectionism also falls within the emotional root of procrastination because it's driven by fears of failure and being uncomfortable in unknown situations. Perfectionists want to know that they'll succeed. They need to know that they can score the best results on their exams, be the employee of the month at work, and impress other people with their skills.

They are foiled by self-doubt when they face a new challenge, even if adversities are an expected part of life. These people will rather avoid the risks involved than take a stand for themselves. Perfectionists are ultimately driven by their emotions. Other emotional problems with procrastination arise when people become rebellious. They've allowed their emotions to take center stage for too long and just rebel against trying. Some people suffer from indecisiveness due to depression and anxiety as well. There's a deep level of uncertainty involved in making decisions and this can lead to procrastination.

Depressed and anxious people are suffering from chemical imbalances in the brain which cause their emotions to influence the subconscious mind before logic can take over. It's not something they do intentionally either. Then we get the people who feel vulnerable to the task at hand. It requires them to step out of their comfort zones and this leads to erratic fears. However, emotions are simply a precursor. The best thing we can do with them is to acknowledge and accept them. That will give us the upper hand over procrastination. Bringing logic back into our minds will automatically take care of them.

The main cause for concern with delay tactics lies in the second root. The second origin of your procrastination could stem from a complicated relationship with time itself.

Some people call procrastinators "wishful thinkers." This isn't hard to believe because every time you postpone a task, you're thinking wishfully and not logically. People who have issues with time see it as their opponent which they need to outwit. They think they can outmaneuver and outlive time. The formal term for this is disorganized procrastinators. They have no organization in their lives and this leads to problems that can start the cycle.

Students and people who work with deadlines are often stuck in the rut of having no organizational skills, which are so important that one would think they'd teach us in school. These people have two clocks in their lives. Their subjective time clashes with the actual time on the mantle clock. The problem is that it becomes nearly impossible to accurately anticipate deadlines, work steadily towards your goals, and allocate the right amount of time you need to complete tasks. People who suffer from this often take on smaller tasks first. They want to complete the simpler tasks and leave the grueling ones for later.

Urgency doesn't play a role in the sequence of tasks they complete. John might think it's simpler to complete his tax returns which are due next month because he's more familiar with it. That's how he pushes the urgent task further away. By the time the urgent task is unavoidable, he's completely overwhelmed by the necessity itself. A common trend in this is when we end up with a pile of urgent tasks and not enough time to complete them. Time management is challenging for disorganized people. This leads to a lack of understanding of the order the tasks need to be completed in.

Disorganized people also have no idea that every task can be broken into smaller challenges. They leave big tasks for last because they cannot see how the project can be divided into more manageable sections. Other people will see the newest task as the most urgent. This means that John focuses on new tasks and experiences he needs to get through instead of returning to his urgent presentation. It doesn't matter how insignificant these new tasks are: he will prioritize them so that he can momentarily escape his work. We also see this behavior in people with attention deficit disorder because they can't maintain focus on the task at hand. Unfortunately, these people spread themselves thin and it becomes impossible for them to finish everything on time.

Disorganized people also suffer from memory issues while at the same time thinking they have an elephant's memory. They expect themselves to remember every task, meeting, assignment, and social responsibility for the next month. They don't realize that they're only human and forgetfulness is a real threat. The world requires us to move fast and multitask, but we aren't always capable of this, even if we think we are. This only compounds the procrastinators' troubles when they finally realize they have too much on their plates. One would think this would slow down the disorganized trend, but it only strengthens the circle further.

The Justifications

The fact that our subconscious minds are responsible for controlling our behaviors is the reason we need to understand where the justifications come from. Excuses are known as cognitive distortions in psychology: it means that we have a certain bias in our brains that has been installed habitually over time. Biases are built upon years of taught behavior and thought processes. Cognitive is another word for higher thinking or logical processing. Distortions is another word for a mistake in our logical processes. We make excuses based on illogical thought processes.

This doesn't mean that there's something actually wrong with a procrastinator's brain. It simply means that they must identify which distortions their bias is grounded in so that they can change them. That's why emotional roots aren't as important because once we regain control of our logic, we regain control of our time.

We'll have a look at the six most common distortions.

The first one is called *denial* or *trivialization*. This describes anyone who advertently believes that delayed behavior isn't actually procrastination. These people will justify their procrastination, by all means necessary, because they believe that their behavior is normal, and for example that the new task or opportunity was more important than the presentation at work or the assignment at school. Even keeping in mind that more urgent tasks can come your way as we've mentioned before, we cannot say that having beers with a friend was more important than finishing the presentation.

We can't think that finishing our taxes ahead of time is more crucial than completing a project we get paid for that's due tomorrow. Anyone who justifies their priorities on emotions rather than logic suffers from denial or trivialization. Our pressing tasks aren't trivial. You wouldn't be reading this right now if they were. People in denial will even convince themselves that there's no pressure to complete the task when the deadline looms over their heads.

The second distortion is called *distraction.* Let's face it, distractions are easy to come by and tempting to partake in. The truth is that anyone who immerses themselves in other behaviors or actions to prevent awareness of the task which must be done is avoiding the obvious. They'll do anything to avoid working on what they need to be doing. Some people use distractions that might seem logical, or at least they try to make it rational by helping someone with a pressing issue.

Ben's deadline is drawing nearer as he has three days left until he needs to deliver, yet when his colleague is struggling to do a spreadsheet on the computer, he will spend hours teaching him how to use formulas to avoid his task. Ben goes home and is called by a friend who broke his leg. He rushes to the hospital even though his friend assured him that he has loads of support. Ben is looking for distractions without realizing it. He would rather spend hours at the hospital than face his presentation.

The third distortion is called *the descending counter factuality*. This is another method in which your brain fools you into believing the rationality behind irrational behavior. Ben might've noticed that he has an issue with meeting deadlines as he reaches the truth step in the circle. Now he starts looking for excuses to downplay his actions. He starts comparing his procrastination behavior to someone else's worse situation. He might even make a pro and con list in his head comparing his delayed behavior to Alex at work.

He looks at Alex's situation and thinks that his boss is more likely to get rid of the less valuable employees by starting with someone who can't even work on spreadsheets. Yes, he missed his deadlines but Alex didn't even know what a formula was. How could the two of them possibly compare? This is how Ben's mind starts justifying his behavior. He looks at other people's problems to shrink his own. This comparison can lead to issues, such as when Ben is called in for disciplinary action due to a notable lack of interest in his work. He'll have a hard time talking his way out of his problems when he tries to blame Alex for his shortfalls.

The fourth distortion is called *valorization.* This is another self-satisfying habit where we tell ourselves that it's okay if we missed a deadline because we accomplished so much elsewhere. Unfortunately, elsewhere doesn't always save our backsides when we are fired or lose our homes. Valorization is like trying to convince the bank not to take your home because you have an irrelevant reason for missing a payment. You were busy helping your grandmother shop for groceries on your day off, and that's why you missed the payment.

I can guarantee you that the bank will not accept this excuse. The same applies to a student walking into class and telling their teacher all about their weekend's irrelevant achievements. So, what if they went ziplining and helped their dad build a new soapbox car. They were supposed to do their homework regardless of any other responsibilities. Valorization is the internal conflict you have with yourself when you assure yourself that missing the deadline is fine because of all the irrelevant achievements you earned in the meantime.

The fifth distortion is called *blaming*. Procrastinators who find any excuse that translates to "out of my control" fall within this category. Indeed, things happen beyond our control but this distortion is as old as the well-known "the dog ate my homework" excuse. The problem with this one is that only you'll know the truth. Some people will say that they were late because they left their phone at home. That's not your partner's problem. You knew you committed but you forgot your phone. This can be true or made-up. You need to be honest with yourself about whether you might've intentionally forgotten your phone.

Other people will blame their service provider for the fact that their emails never came through. This is seemingly out of someone's control, but anyone who waits for email instructions from their boss should be checking on their signal regularly. Other excuses in the same line are "I had my phone on silent" and "I was swamped with responsibilities at home and forgot about my deadline." This person will look for any external force to blame instead of acknowledging that they shouldn't have their phone on silent.

The last distortion is called *mocking* because it involves someone using humor to validate their procrastination. Humor is a great ice-breaker but there comes a time when we must own up to our mistakes and not turn everything into a joke. Many procrastinators will think it's hilarious that they missed their appointment at the doctor or left their friend alone at the restaurant without canceling. The truth is that people won't enjoy a joke when they've been disappointed. The other side of this is when you turn your problem with delay tactics into a self-justification in your mind.

These procrastinators laugh about missing their bus when they were expected to deliver a presentation at work. This distortion also acts as a coping mechanism for delayers when they refuse to admit to their behaviors, which can only turn sour because laughing about losing our jobs won't get them back either.

Part 2:

Action Plan

As promised, we can finally dive into the exercises that will change your life for the better. You've learned about where procrastination originates and how it controls your decisions. You know that procrastinating can have serious consequences in any area of your life. You also know that there's a cycle that happens below our conscious awareness. Now it's time to break the cycle and take action against the habit that's held you back from being the greatest version of yourself. This section will teach you how to break the shackles and move forward with simple exercises. Habits are the enemy but they needn't be anymore.

Chapter 4:

Change is a Process

We must start changing our procrastination behavior by understanding it thoroughly. Our brains are capable of so much, but they're also prone to certain issues. Procrastination is anything but laziness. Change is a neural process that requires a gradual shift and not a forceful shove over the edge. This chapter will help you understand how habits are formed in our brains and the various motions they go through before they become engraved into us. We must be aware of the steps we need to take so that we don't blindly set foot in the wrong direction. Changing habits, rebuilding them, and removing unwanted habits will become much simpler and more straightforward.

Behavioral Stages

People think that changing our ways is as easy as a hot knife slicing through butter. It can be, but rushing into things will only set you further back. Baby steps are required to reach the goalposts. Addressing behavioral changes must go through five essential stages or we'll undoubtedly fail. James Prochaska, a professor of psychology at Rhode Island University, recognized five stages we must go through (Webb, 2016).

The first stage is called *precontemplation*, also better known as denial. Procrastinators are stuck at this stage. This is the phase where we deny the existence of procrastination, so there's no immediate decision to make changes. "Procrastination, what are you talking about?" These people haven't notably suffered any consequences from their behavior yet. They might be enlightened to their problem by family, friends, or colleagues; however, this doesn't always work. Someone in this phase isn't ready to consciously recognize their behavior. They are probably not even thinking about it unless someone mentions it. They can also be a little offended when someone points their behavior out.

The second stage of procrastination is called *contemplation*. This is often triggered by consequences or successful social enlightenment. Although, it's hardly ever the latter kind of enlightenment. Thoughts and actions will begin surfacing whether procrastinators are ready to change this or not. They'll also start thinking about how to deal with the changes and the repercussions that may come, both negative or positive. However, this person still isn't fully ready to proceed. They'll consciously confirm that they procrastinate, but they'll delay actions until tomorrow. "I know I put things off and it's led to unwanted consequences, but tomorrow is another day." This is fine because the person is starting to become aware of their behavior, which is a step further from denial.

The third stage of change is called *preparation*. Preparation doesn't necessarily include change itself, but it's when the person starts being more open to new ideas. They'll test the waters as they become more willing to try new things. "Okay, I'll finally start trying to finish my work on time", or "Okay, I'll begin working on my relationship because it's only getting worse." The notable problem with this stage is that the procrastinator is willing but won't commit just yet. They might even see some progress on new habits they try, but they aren't dedicated yet.

The fourth stage of changing habits is called *action*. The procrastinator will actively commit to making some changes now. They implement new behaviors, change their environment, and openly experience new things. This stage vastly requires discipline and commitment to stick with new behavior. Prochaska confirms that if we stick to our new routines and rebuilding exercises long enough, we'll benefit from forming new habits. Taking action requires you to be strong and follow through with what you prepared for; however, this stage is closely followed by the fifth one.

The fifth stage is called *maintenance*. This requires us to repeat new behaviors long enough to develop them and make them permanent. The five stages are straightforward, but they can also be broken into additional segments called "processes of change." Processes of change are most significant in the contemplation stage for most people. These segments are the mental shifts that move you closer to the end of the stage itself. Our brains are powerful but they also need smooth transitions.

The first segment is called *conscious raising*. This means that you must become consciously aware of where you are in the stages and the circumstances surrounding it. Some people keep journals to track their awareness. The second segment is called *self-reevaluation*. This is when you would take notes of the behaviors you need to change and the consequences that come from them. We call this a mental t-chart. It's when you start weighing the pros and cons of your choices. The first segment will be clarified throughout the exercises in this book. The second one has already started taking place in your brain as you started evaluating your level of procrastination.

Habits

Habits and behaviors are slightly different. The word behavior only focuses on one aspect of habits, whereas habits themselves are a consecutive sequence of events in our minds. We'll focus on learning more about what habits are and how they're formed mentally, subconsciously, and neurologically. Many people fail at changing habits because they think it's purely a behavioral issue. This is wrong because habits are a looped sequence of four aspects. We go through the loop within a split second. Emotions and thoughts are part of the process but the best way to understand how to halt the process is to learn about the four aspects in the sequence. Keep in mind that this is a biological process that starts from birth.

The first sequence is called the *cues.* Our brains are constantly collecting data and trying to make sense of the world around us. Cues are the stimuli that start the process in our minds: they set off a motion that relates to a reward. These rewards can be primal or natural, such as needing food, water, and sleep. Secondary rewards also surface: these include financial or social satisfaction, fame, approval, love, power, and status. Our brains look for memorable rewards to match with the cues we experience. Someone who starts a new project at work or school might be triggered with fear because they don't think they can achieve approval in the end.

The second sequence is called the *cravings.* Unfortunately, cravings are a motivational drive for the habit loop. These words have been tied to sugar, nicotine, and caffeine, but many people don't understand that their brain automatically switches to cravings after a cue of any kind. This also doesn't mean that it desires the behavior or action itself. It indicates a desire for the satisfaction that comes after the behavior. People aren't motivated by skipping their responsibilities, but rather by the relief they feel during the response itself. For example, Sam feels stressed by his project at work, so he needs a mental and emotional release from this feeling by watching something on Netflix instead of finishing his work. Unfortunately, the relief is short-lived and his stress is worse after the fact.

His brain is thinking irrationally, convincing him that the temporary relief will help him cope better while forgetting about the long-term consequences.

The third sequence is our *behavior* or *response.* Responses are actions and thoughts. You think that watching a show on Netflix will reward you, so you respond physically. It's also important to know that there are factors that come with a response. Your brain is less likely to respond when more effort is required. It will evaluate the steps required to carry out the action or thought before it instructs you physically. The response also depends on your abilities because if you aren't capable of following the instructions, the brain won't bother. Yes, every person on earth has this process in their brains and are predisposed to laziness. Any task that requires too much energy will automatically become a distant thought.

The fourth sequence is called the *rewards.* Rewards are there to satisfy your craving and relieve tension, stress, and discomfort. In our example, Sam's reward is streaming hours of Netflix. He's soothing his stress and curbing the urges inside of his mind. Rewards can be our best friends or our worst enemies, depending on the frequency of our negative behavior. We can achieve our goals of getting a promotion at work, which acts as a powerful reward, but we can also feel a biological reward from lazing on the couch. This loop happens from the time of birth because every time we experience pleasure or reward, however briefly, it engraves the habit into our minds.

Our brains know that certain cravings can be satisfied with specific rewards, even if they're harmful. This is how the habit or feedback loop continues in our brains. Targeting one process won't help you eradicate the problem. Your brain is like a child who throws a tantrum for candy. It will get what it wants because it prefers to retain reward information that requires the least amount of work. To summarize, we must see a challenging task at work as the cue. Then we crave the need to relieve the frustration brewing inside of us. The response is the act of browsing social media or watching TV instead of working. The reward comes from the temporary relief felt which solidifies the loop.

Penetrating the Loop

Rewards or incentives are at the core of what triggers our cues, drives our cravings, and makes us behave a certain way. We can unbuild a habit by replacing negative rewards with relative ones among other strategies. Our brains are always looking for a reward and this would be the best place to start. Psychiatrist and neuroscientist Judson Brewer is the director of research and innovation at the Brown University Mindfulness Center, and he explains that we can target habit changes with alternative rewards (Winkowski, 2019). The procrastination loop will continue unless we interrupt it by giving it something better to do.

Avoidance has been a common habit for procrastinators. It acts as a reward to relieve frustration and stress, but it leads to endless problems. Doctor Brewer expresses the value of offering your brain a "bigger, better offer" to change your mind. People tend to concern themselves about the present moment rather than their future wellbeing. Our minds tend to live in the present and our future selves can seem like strangers. That's why your brain prefers immediate relief even when it leads to consequences. Thinking of our future wellbeing is the only time we allow our minds to travel forward. Nevertheless, we must feed our cravings for pleasure with a swift alternative that rewards our future selves. Cravings are an addiction and any addict will tell you how hard it is to persuade the mind to think of anything else.

It's not impossible though, but we must give our brains what they want. There are so many substitute options that are often more negative and that's why we must internalize our change. However, focusing solely on your deep desire for relief isn't the only way of rebuilding a habit. We need to focus on the entire loop, including the cues, cravings, responses, and rewards. The first thing you do is recognize why you're procrastinating by keeping all four factors in mind. You realize that the task stresses you out because you've never handled a presentation on your own before. How can you change the cue? How can you change the craving and response?

You can start by being kind and compassionate with yourself. Stop beating yourself up because this doesn't change the loop. Forgive yourself for procrastinating because dwelling on this will only keep you in it. We can become more productive by practicing self-compassion. Procrastination and its consequences are something we can't change: we can only focus on ridding ourselves of it in the future. Learn to become familiar with your future self. Being hard on yourself only succeeds in increasing your stress, which will act as a buffer for more procrastination. It's engraving those loops deeper into your mind. Self-compassion can also enhance your motivation and self-growth in the long run.

Another way of combating the sudden urge to procrastinate is to turn it into a curious moment. We can do this by shifting our attention to the feelings and sensations in our minds and bodies when it strikes. Increase your awareness as you start sorting through the reasons why you stopped. What is tempting you and where can you feel it in your body? Are you hungry or is it just your mind's trickery to delay work? Allow your mind to momentarily slip back to previous procrastination and feel the similarity in the loop. Focus intensely on the urge to procrastinate as you take note of whether it's diminishing, magnifying, or stirring emotions. Awareness can often calm these feelings down before they erupt.

We can also prevent ourselves from giving in to the urge by planning our next action strategically. This isn't the same as breaking your task into smaller bits. We must focus solely on the next action and nothing beyond it. This form of self-deception can calm our nerves when we're stressed. The trick to this is to pretend as though the next action is only a possibility. Think of this as acting to some extent. Ask yourself what you would do next if you started the project. However, you're pretending as though you're not going to proceed. Some people experience a paradox where they find themselves acting out their thoughts when they do this. Motivation is quite versatile and it can also follow an action.

Another way to convince your mind to forget about procrastinating is to make the task less convenient. Complicate the automatic response so that you can replace it with a more convenient option. The brain is biologically lazy even if we won't admit it. The harder it is to procrastinate, the less likely you will be to do it. You can call a colleague to keep you accountable. You can even ask them to help you with the presentation to make the alternative more convenient. You'll worry about getting into trouble if you don't finish the task once your colleague holds you accountable. You can then make all the procrastination cues inconvenient. Do you want to watch a movie instead? Pack your television away so that you need to go through the schlep of unpacking it.

This strategy helps us change our environmental cues. Most people prefer the easier route rather than having to unpack their TV while they also can't remember where they hid the remote control. Complicate the temptations as much as you can. You need to place obstacles or challenges between you and the procrastination habit to make the urge go away. This also works on diminishing the reward because the gratification seems further away. Keep in mind that your loop functions on your desires. Making the desires less attractive will get you started. You can even enlist some friends to help you too. It's far simpler to remain on target when you're doing this collaboratively with friends, family, or colleagues. You can ask them to check in with you in a couple of hours to see how you've progressed.

The final strategy is to feed your urges with a relatable alternative. We must give in to the urges by replacing one reward with another. This can be done short term by promising yourself a night out with friends if you manage to get your project done. Make sure your new reward is within immediate reach as well or this attempt could fail. You can focus on working until seven tonight and then meet your friends instead of spending two hours watching Netflix now and working through the night. This is the swift switch-up. Long-term reward replacement is also possible when you get the hang of things. Keep self-compassion in mind as you decide how much work needs to be done before you reach a reward.

Perhaps, your laptop is as old as time itself and you can get a new one if you dedicate an hour every night to sorting out your paperwork. Make sure the alternative reward is as exciting as the old one. There are three secrets to making any of these strategies work long enough to engrave new loops. Your awareness will help you decide why you want the change. Knowing why you need change is an essential step. Secondly, baby steps cannot be emphasized enough. You can't decide to lose weight by shocking your body into submission because your brain will retaliate. Work your way towards larger goals gradually. Replace one day a week with new eating habits and focus on the real reason why you want to reach your goal. You don't care about your closet shrinking as much as you care about your dating life.

Finally, don't try to change five habits at once. Focus on one at a time until you have it and then move onto the next. A bonus secret is to make sure you love the new habit. Don't choose changes that send your brain into self-destruct mode either.

This chapter has laid the groundwork on habits. The next few chapters will focus on the negative emotions associated with procrastination and how we can offer our brains an emotionally healthier, alternative reward.

Chapter 5:

Identify: A Procrastination Inventory

It's time to move you from the contemplation phase into the preparation stage. We must use the processes of change to get your mindset ready for the changes ahead. This includes becoming fully aware of your habits and evaluating yourself thoroughly. If you can learn to identify your unwanted behaviors and excuses, you can more easily learn to let go of them and aim for a mindset of growth. You must learn from your behavior and practice positive change.

Acceptance

Many procrastinators only lack discipline in certain aspects of their lives. Some are the greatest romantic partners, but can't hold down a job. Others are always handing their work in before their deadlines, but they fell out of the self-care tree and hit every branch on the way down.

Richard was one of the worst cases I've had the unfortunate pleasure of witnessing. Richard was the pinnacle of a defier. He lived by the typical "my way or the highway" motto. He was always getting into trouble for missing his project deadlines, but it had nothing to do with his intelligence. In fact, he was top of the class when he handed in his work. He became smug to prove that he could still perform, but he would only do it at his leisure. The problem was that his defiant behavior gradually collided with another procrastination style.

Soon enough, he was a collision of a defier and crisis-maker procrastinator before he even finished high school. Unfortunately, he remained unaware inside the precontemplation stage. Even I tried to enlighten him because he was my friend, but I was also becoming disheartened by his nonchalant attitude towards keeping his promises. Nonetheless, the first time he took a major blow was when he was offered a scholarship at university and his defiant behavior bit him in the backside. He just had to turn his procrastination into a life-altering crisis. Richard failed to hand the necessary documents on time and missed out on the financial aid he needed. He could have applied again a year later, but his procrastination took a deep nosedive instead.

Why should he attend university now? He echoed this question in our social group. He thought it would okay to attend university at a later age. He wanted to live his life first. Unsurprisingly, Richard ended up with the bottom of the barrel jobs. It wasn't long before he was fired and got another pathetic job. His life continued like this for a few years. I'll never forget his beaten-up truck either. It was a gamble every time he traveled to see his girlfriend in the next county. The check engine light was flashing endlessly. It was no surprise that it would often break down in the middle of nowhere. However, Richard pushed his luck around every corner. He thought his truck could go another 10,000 miles before it needed a service. He also thought his landlord could wait another month while he looked for a new job after being fired again. Richard entered this endless procrastination cycle.

It was the day I found him crying next to his truck that I realized he had finally reached the next phase. Contemplation surfaced as he recognized his faults. Richard was a rare kind of procrastinator. He wasn't prone to minor procrastination; his entire life was a delay tactic. He lost his apartment, his fifth girlfriend, and every job for five years straight. Fortunately, most procrastinators aren't like this at all. They tend to falter in one area of their lives and function at high speeds in another.

The point is that you need to take an inventory of your life. You need to realize where you procrastinate, what excuses you use, and how it's affected yourself and others. The first thing you must do in this exercise is to think of two to three procrastination experiences you can best recall. Break these experiences down and ask yourself questions to better understand what happened.

What happened during the delayed actions?

Who was involved with the procrastination?

What led up to the moment I delayed actions?

How did I feel about what happened?

What was the outcome of my decisions?

Did my actions hurt or inconvenience anyone else?

Can I identify any patterns or common themes of procrastination?

What was I afraid of when I avoided the experience or task?

The answers you find will also help you recognize the consequences that are personal to you. You can also see if you're hurting other people by delaying everything. I know that Richard's parents were deeply hurt by their son who refused to listen to anyone for 30 years. However, the answers can also reveal your inner fears and the inner critic that whispers perceived failure to you. You'll identify more than fear because all the emotions will surface when you take the time to focus on these incidents. Disappointment, anger, physical pain, depression, guilt, anxiety, dread, denial, and feelings of incompetence are all internal consequences that affect you emotionally.

You can also lose interest in previous activities, feel fraudulent, exhausted, stressed, suffer from brain fog, humiliation, embarrassment, and alienation. The external consequences could include the loss of finances, jobs, social and romantic relationships, academic performance, and opportunities. You could also note a decreased working responsibility, tense relationships with your colleagues and boss, marital problems, and divorce. Your credit rating can go out of the window and you can lose your home and car. You might've even succumbed to accidents or injuries.

Take some time and make notes of what your consequences have been.

Further Evidence

You must continue delving into your procrastination. Keep the types in mind as you work through the areas of your life where you struggle. Are you a perfectionist who puts tasks off out of fear of not achieving perfect results? Are you a dreamer who isn't great at paying attention to detail because your mind wanders off? Are you the defier who doesn't allow people to dictate your schedules and deadlines? Are you the crisis-maker who seems to thrive off of the adrenalin involved in delaying tasks until the last minute? Are you the worrier who fears change because the unknown is too scary? Or are you the overdoer who burns the candle at both ends when you take on more than you can handle?

Now it's time to see which areas of your life are most affected by procrastination loops. You can see which examples relate to you and give yourself a score for each category's intensity. This will help you choose the most pressing areas because you know that habits must be changed one at a time.

Home Examples

Do you fail to keep up with the regular chores, such as washing dishes, laundry, yard maintenance, cleaning, and changing the kitty litter?

Have you put off any home repairs or projects that you started?

Do you delay calling the handyman, repairman, landscaper, cleaner, or contractor?

Have you delayed any repairs to your vehicles?

Do you struggle to keep up with your paperwork, such as collecting the mail?

Have you ever found it impossible to make decisions in the home?

How often do you run short of groceries when you persistently delay your shopping?

Do you find time to declutter your home or garage?

Are there any unpacked moving boxes and how long have they been there?

Have you postponed upgrading your security at home?

Workplace Examples

This section includes paid and volunteer work.

How often are you late to work or meetings?

Have you struggled to find time to learn new skills or implement new ideas?

Do you struggle with making decisions, or handling calls, emails, and text messages?

Do you often skip on your administrative responsibilities?

How often do you delay presentations and deadlines?

Do you avoid confronting or complimenting someone at work?

Has your paperwork fallen behind?

Have you ever postponed asking for a promotion or raise?

Have you every delayed career redirection or networking?

School Examples

How often are you late for classes?

Do you struggle to deliver homework, assignments, and presentations in on time?

Do you study at the last minute?

Do you postpone talking to lecturers, professors, and advisors?

Have you failed to apply for financial aid as Richard did?

Do you put off payments to the college or school?

Have you struggled to choose a major?

Did you postpone calling home?

Have you avoided employment and internship searches?

Have you delayed applying for a special program you wanted to do?

Personal Care Examples

Do you avoid exercising or losing weight?

Do you break promises made to yourself to quit smoking or drinking?

Are you nonchalant with your medical appointments?

How often do you delay your prescription refills?

Do you postpone haircuts or brushing your teeth?

How often do you shop for new clothing or clean out your closet for goodwill?

Do you ever make enough time to pursue hobbies and interests?

Have you procrastinated on educational, spiritual, and other meaningful activities?

How often do you take a vacation?

Are you capable of making long-term decisions?

Social Examples

Do you stay in contact with friends and family?

Have you put off asking someone on a date?

Do you ever invite people into your home?

Have you ever avoided recreational activities with your social group?

Do you struggle to express or accept compliments?

Are you known as the late-comer at social gatherings?

Have you ever postponed a conversation with a friend or partner?

How often do you ask for help when you need it?

Are you capable of ending a poor relationship?

Financial Examples

Do you file your taxes on time?

Are you disorganized with receipts and tax records?

Do you struggle with establishing a budget and tracking your expenses?

Have you ever delayed fruitful investment opportunities?

Do you postpone contact with banks and creditors to solve problems?

Have you ever paid your mortgage, rent, credit cards, or other bills late?

Do you avoid paying parking tickets until your car is towed away?

Do you procrastinate on collecting debts owed to you?

Have you postponed insurance claims?

This should give you a great idea of where you must start. These are the most common procrastination behaviors in these categories. List your delay tactics from worst to minor so that you can prioritize which need changes first.

Excuses Galore

The final part of the inventory exercise is to identify how many excuses you make. What do you say to yourself when you delay something? How does this somehow justify not doing what you need to do? The best way to discover your excuses is to pay attention to the moment you procrastinate. Your mind will find a reason why putting the task off until a later time is acceptable. We can start focusing on the incidents you've chosen that came with consequences. Work through this list and never stop adding to it as you notice problematic justification patterns. There are a few common excuses that we must look out for.

"I've got to get organized first because I don't have everything I need." This comes at a time when you're feeling unprepared for the task at hand, so your mind is trying to convince you that something's amiss. A feeling of disorganization shows you that you're afraid of making a mistake. Doctor Jane Burka and Lenora Yuen explain that we must focus on our thoughts and emotions during this excuse in their book *Procrastination: Why You Do it, What to Do About It* (Burka & Yuen, 2008).

"I don't have time to finish this now, so there's no point in starting anyway. Besides, it's a wonderful day and it shouldn't be wasted on this." Wishful thinking is rife here because every day is a beautiful day in truth. Honestly, how will you know how much you're capable of unless you start? Also, what if tomorrow is an even better day?

"I've worked so damn hard that I deserve a break." There's no argument when it comes to someone who needs a break, but there's a time and place for everything. Breaks should be strategically planned according to your responsibilities. It's part of self-care and can be useful, but someone who echoes this frequently is looking for excuses.

"My project won't be good enough, so why bother?" This self-defeating excuse can do more harm than good in the long run. You might be a perfectionist if you're experiencing this excuse often enough. Once again, you won't know how good you are until you try. You might surprise yourself by designing a show-stopping presentation.

"I can do my best if I wait and work under pressure." Understandably, many active procrastinators rely on this excuse, but we cannot predict the future. Firstly, the body isn't made to work under constant pressure. Secondly, you don't know if you'll have the time to do it later. Something more pressing could arise or opportunities could come your way.

"I won't start writing my thesis until I'm inspired." Inspiration is just like time; it waits for no man or woman. We can't guarantee that it will come but this makes for a convenient excuse. The truth is that it's easier to make small changes to a project than to start it from the beginning.

"I feel unwell, tired, or my mood is miserable today." Unfortunately, these make up the most common excuses. This is also the easiest way to justify procrastination because you think you can predict your mood, energy, and health tomorrow. We forget that tomorrow can be more challenging. Your unwanted mood might deprive you of sleep and cause you to feel exhausted tomorrow.

"I can do this in no time, and there's still plenty of time left." This is another fallacy that springs to mind to convince us that we know exactly what the future holds. We think we can complete the task in two hours, but why do we fear to start it then? This excuse is a distorted one that helps people overestimate their abilities and underestimate the project or time required to finish it.

"I'm enjoying myself so much right now that I'll regret leaving." No doubt leaving an exciting experience with one friend to meet another is hard. The problem is that you're breaking a promise and the consequences can be much worse than missing out on a bit of fun. You can lose a friend who needed you and you left them hanging dry.

"I need to feed myself, sleep, or exercise before I start." This is another typical avoidance excuse. Segregating your efforts might not lead to desired results. We must eat when we're hungry and we must exercise to keep ourselves healthy. However, you need to prioritize your tasks. Besides, eating something takes five minutes. There's no need for an hour in front of social media while you eat. Multitasking the primal act of eating while working is possible too.

There are so many excuses you can use that it's difficult to mention them all. See how many common excuses you relate to and make a list of them.

"The task is so important that I need to give it more thought and attention. I can do this better tomorrow when my mind is clear."

"The task isn't that important and can wait until I'm done with another one."

"This task is way too difficult to manage at once, therefore, I'll spend more time on it tomorrow, irrespective of the deadline."

"I don't have enough time to work on this today, and I magically know that I'll have more time tomorrow."

"It's not the right time to do this now."

"I'm not gifted, talented, or skilled enough for this."

"I'm waiting for someone else's help."

"My friend needs me so I'll put off my work for her."

"Why should I try if the answer will only be no anyway?"

"I've finished the hard part and now I can take a break before I slide into the home stretch."

Chapter 6:

Time to Do it NOW

You have your inventory in place and you can now move into the exercises that will stop the procrastination loop. This chapter will focus on what you shouldn't do while teaching you about a valuable technique that is more powerful than you know. Chances are that you'll procrastinate on the idea, but as soon as you dive in, you'll see how it gets easier. Remember that practice will make perfect when it comes to changing habits. The good news is that there's a five-minute exercise that can trump those delay tactics. Five minutes doesn't seem threatening, right? That's the idea because procrastinators will avoid difficult tasks, especially in the beginning. Using swift and simple techniques will give you the nudge you need to start laying the foundation of new habits.

Breaking Myths

Allow us to discredit a myth that only harms people before you jump into the exercise. Popular sneaker brand Nike has turned our attention to their logo with the echo of "just do it." This has led to many people, coaches, and uninformed individuals claiming that we can *just do it* and get over the procrastination we suffer from. I agree that the best way to remove delay tactics is to start the project you fear. The problem is that too many of the advocates who tell us to *just do it* are unfamiliar with the loop you learned about. There are too many factors involved to simply jump into the deep end of something we fear.

If life was as simple as the Nike motto makes it sound, we wouldn't need advice on overcoming this problem. You wouldn't be reading this book and I wouldn't be writing it. The slogan is unrealistic and deceptive at best. It might sound good in theory and it may seemingly resonate with a solution, but the unstructured idea is rarely sufficient enough to do the job. Procrastination habits will often be the victor in the showdown. The rare instances where it works temporarily is when your boss or spouse gives you an ultimatum. Either *just do it*, or you can look for a new job. *Just do it* or you can sign divorce papers tomorrow.

Some procrastinators are more likely to follow through when threatened; however, this can also negatively impact you. You're emotionally damaged after this and delay tactics will become more prevalent. Nevertheless, the *just do it* mantra is highly unlikely to get reasonable things done without a delay. It's as effective as the "just say no" campaigns that try to teach kids and teenagers to say no to drugs and alcohol. These adverts have never attained the results they were intended to get.

Focusing on Facts

Contrary to the *just do it* attitude, the "do it now" concept is based on psychology and realistic ideations. The "just do it" myth has no structure, whereas the timeous *do it now* method can help you defeat this habit. The structure provides the groundwork for preventing misinterpretations and consequent mistakes. The *do it now* process is explained as getting reasonable things done reasonably within a realistic time frame. I know that's a mouthful but it increases your overall effectiveness, efficiency, and satisfaction with life. I know that asking someone to *do it now* when they feel like retracting into their shell is tough, but overcoming procrastination will be an obstacle.

Think of it as hurdles you need to jump over. The further along the track you get, the lower the hurdles will be. You can't believe how empowering it feels to shed the procrastination loop from your mind. It will give you back control over your life and things will become less complicated with time. Your confidence will aim for the stars if you persist. However, we must start at the beginning before we can shoot for the stars. Mentally declaring your freedom from procrastination won't help you win the race, but becoming the master of your delay tactics and turning them into an active scenario, will give you a chance of winning the marathon.

The truth to why the *just do it* myth fails so often is because it has no structure, time frame, or measurable distance. Okay, so we must *just do it*, but what do we expect ourselves to do? How much time do we give ourselves to get to what point? The beauty of structure is that we can measure our smaller steps. We can also feel less resistance when we make it simpler. Small strides will help us accomplish a greater scheme when we look back. *Just doing it* indicates that we must tackle the mammoth task we fear without flinching. Have you seen what happens to an amateur boxer who steps in the ring with a famous giant? They'll get pummeled for sure.

However, if that boxer dedicates frequent training sessions before he shows up for the match, he'll stand a greater chance at success, and he might even become the new champion. He'll start by setting a schedule; one that doesn't frighten him either if he's a procrastinator. You've learned about the influence fears can have on you. You also know that we can remove the power procrastination has over us by simplifying tasks. We can't always see the progress we make when we do tiny things, but they collectively start gaining momentum and we end up with a massive shift into the action and maintenance phases of changing the loop.

You might be wondering how you overcome the motivational gap in the loop by deciding to *do it now*. We've briefly mentioned how motivation can also recede actions in chapter four. Doctor Clifford Lazarus from the Lazarus Institute explains that people are mistaken when they think motivation must precede actions (Lazarus, 2010). Actions can also ignite motivation when you complete a fraction of your goals, whether it's a task, conversation, or attending to a responsibility. Getting closer to the goalposts will ignite motivation inside of you. You won't feel motivated at first, but if you commit yourself to five minutes of doing something, it will lead to another five minutes.

The minutes don't always have to run consecutively either. My friend Richard started with five minutes on and five minutes off. However, he was a rare case of exceptionally difficult procrastination habits. Nevertheless, every five minutes you complete will amplify your motivation as you start realizing that you've accomplished something rather than nothing. Compare your five minutes of action to a stone dropped in a lake. Now keep dropping stones in the lake and watch the ripple effects cross each other. Suddenly, there's a momentum growing and the water looks stormy. You want to become the eye of the hurricane in the fighting ring of life.

Humans are also prone to pride and when you continue surprising yourself, you'll find an increasing interest to want more. There's no need to rush this exercise either. You don't have to follow through with it every time you stagger a little. Also, don't expect yourself to be in charge of your motivation after a week of practicing it. Keep in mind that the loop can only be redirected permanently if you persistently practice the *do it now* method until it becomes automatic. The maintenance stage of forming a new habit is a gradual and steady incline. You have to change your thoughts with consistency, but don't knock your head against the wall when you stumble. Forgive yourself compassionately and move on.

Otherwise, you're procrastinating on guilt and self-blame again. We need to adopt a "tit for tat" attitude to commit to the *do it now* method. Think about the procrastination loop for a moment. You've just encountered a cue and your brain is craving the delayed actions that will relieve anxiety. The cue might be when your boss hands you a new project at work and gives you a strict deadline. The cravings are telling you to do everything but start the project because this will help you clear your mind, prepare yourself, research, and relax before the race towards the deadline. This is when you need to immediately implement what we call the *tit for tat strategy*.

Keep in mind that your looping response is both thoughtful and actionable. We don't do anything without thinking. You need to interrupt your train of thoughts before you physically act them out. This won't always be possible in the beginning but practice will make it easier. Many procrastination thoughts are irrational or automatic, and we call them "task interfering thoughts" or TITs. We must move our minds into "task activating thoughts" or TATs instead. A TIT is an excuse or justification that slips into your mind faster than you can blink. It's the same inner dialogue that's telling you to postpone working on the project until tomorrow because you're so tired today. You somehow know that you'll feel better tomorrow and think you can tackle it head-on.

These intrusive thoughts can also include any of the other excuses you make. The activating thought is one that you're going to give as an alternative. The trick with this is that it must entice you. Remember that we're focusing on the entire loop for maximum results. Become your own interrogator for a moment before you proceed. Ask yourself what alternative, activating thought would be more rewarding in the near future. You can delay the project until tomorrow but that means that you can't meet with friends on Sunday because you'll be working.

Weigh the pros and cons of the rewards for both thoughts. This will be particularly useful if you have something amazing planned. If you don't have plans; call a friend and make some. And please, don't procrastinate on the call either. Planning something amazing will also stir an ounce of motivation inside of you. Another technique we can implement immediately is the "first-things-first" method. This thought disrupting technique allows us to move closer to more urgent tasks. Stop yourself before you continue procrastinating until you identify the most important task in front of you.

Is there any task that's more important and time-restrained to the one you're about to get into? Is there a more pressing task than what you're doing right now? This could help when your boss assigns that presentation to you, and you find yourself acting out the response already. Query your priorities thoroughly, so that you can see the bigger picture. Delve into your rewards from both tasks before you decide. When you ask yourself what's more important, you might steer clear of possible consequences too. Doctor Willem Knaus explains that we can forget important tasks if we delay them too long (2002). Messages become distorted and important factors can get lost.

Remind yourself of these risks while you try to recognize which task is more relevant. You might forget important information your boss explained to you if you delay the project much longer. Awareness of priorities can remind us to rather *do it now*. You can also save time in the end because you won't be procrastinating on the details you forgot. This works on your inconvenience factor again because it will be more difficult to do the project over the weekend when you can't remember what needs to be done or you can't get in touch with your boss.

Your brain will prefer the easier route here and you'll find yourself doing a little work which leads to motivation again. The *first-things-first method* can help us design a new habit around doing the most important tasks first if we use our fear of complications against ourselves. There are various ways of interrupting your response factor in the loop and keeping the other factors in mind while you encourage your brain to proceed with the task. This adds structure to the *do it now* method, but there's more to it than focus and thinking.

The Five-Minute Holy Grail

The five-minute technique is the *do it now* method, but it adds the most important structure for people who struggle to follow through with interrupting their thoughts. Let's face it, procrastinators can convince themselves to interrupt those thoughts time and again. However, if the newly, less complicated option suddenly becomes more difficult because it requires you to spend hours in front of the computer, you'll fail before you even start. Having exercises we can run in our minds within seconds is great, but we must add the final touch now. This will be exceptionally useful for people at the beginning of the change journey.

The *first-things-first* method focuses on helping you find the most relevant task. It can make other tasks seem more complicated, but it can also make the pressing task seem daunting if it requires hours of work. Sadly, the question of relevancy won't always matter when the project requires loads of effort and time. That's where we continue to make the more pressing task attractive by removing further complications. Your only job here is to dedicate five minutes at a time to it. Make a concerted effort to commit to these five minutes and don't think about anything else for that time. The five minutes will end and you can decide whether you'd like to go another five minutes.

If you can get through a few five-minute sessions, your project will start developing before your eyes and motivation will become abundant. All you have to do is schedule your five minutes and *do it now*! Continue doing this until you know that you're done or you have another important commitment. We'll focus on scheduling soon. Besides, your thoughts and emotions will become harder to convince when your brain has had enough. Finally, you can dedicate five minutes to set up your schedule for tomorrow, research, and get other necessities ready to make work easier when you start tomorrow again.

This already gives you a jump-start on your next session. The beauty with the *five-minute do it now* method is that these brief work periods count more than doing nothing. This method has been successful in breaking the loop gradually.

Chapter 7:

Self-Regulation: PURRRR-fect Protocol

Procrastination is a self-regulation, impulse breakdown where you can't control your thoughts and responses to see the bigger picture. I've mentioned how your future self becomes a stranger, and this causes you to struggle with self-regulation. It's become clear that many procrastinators think they can see into the future, but no one can do this. We can only plan for the future in the hopes of experiencing the best outcome. Delayers experience a collapse of this key ability and their 'psychic' abilities convince them that the foreseeable future is fraught with unpleasantry and negativity. This can be true in some cases but most instances are predicted wrongly. The inability to regulate our thoughts and responses lowers our efficiency and we must combat procrastination behavior with the PURRRR protocol to get ahead of this.

How It Works

Stanford professor Albert Bandura explains that we can increase our self-efficacy to improve our self-regulation and regain control (Knaus, 2002). People who have sufficient self-efficacy know that they can organize their life, regulate their actions, and become masters of procrastination. One of the most powerful tools we can use to reach this stage is called the PURRRR technique. The acronym stands for pause, utilize, reflect, reason, respond, and revise. This technique can be implemented during your *do it now* strategy or be used separately.

Nevertheless, this tool will help you keep your *do it now* engine purring comfortably. The secret is to use these simple techniques because procrastinators don't love complicated strategies. The PURRRR method helps you simplify seemingly adverse tasks or experiences. It requires you to change your perspective, position yourself for a new physical response, implement new actions, and adjust accordingly for optimal results. Let's break the technique down for ease of understanding and use.

Pause: The first step is to freeze in your tracks. Bring your brain and that speedy loop to a screeching halt. Ironically, you'll be delaying your procrastination before it proceeds. Stopping this loop suddenly can already establish a hint of control over the subconscious process. However, your mind might resist. Remember that your mind is much like a toddler who doesn't always take instructions well.

It's easy to overlook the pause stage but it's necessary to silence your mind briefly before you start. It's like finally gaining your toddler's attention, which parents know is difficult. There's a trick to preventing yourself from skipping this stage. Tie a rubber band to your wrist and snap it when you need a reminder. This seems harsh but it's an age-old trick that never fails.

Utilize: This step can be complicated at first because it involves you enforcing your control. The truth is that your self-control hasn't vanished from your life; it's simply lying dormant in your mind. This step helps us suppress those cravings that seem so difficult to erase. You need to take a stand and shut those cravings down, even if it's only temporary at first. *Utilize* is the part where you abruptly stop the physical procrastination behavior.

Imagine yourself having a superpower: freezing time. Now you're freezing the actions that were taking place and not just your mind. You suppress impulsiveness every day without consciously being aware of it. You utilized this seemingly dormant skill when you avoided an incident after stopping at a red light. Your impulses were telling you to go, but you took control. Resist the impulse to move your body further.

Reflect: The third stage of the PURRRR protocol tells you to think about what's happening at the moment. Reflect on what's going on in your mind. What are you imagining? What are you doing? How do you feel right now? Try to identify exactly what the habit loop is craving before you continue. You should be able to understand why it's craving this too. Are you actively avoiding a task that installs fear in you? Are you avoiding interaction with a potential date because you're nervous?

Start gathering information that will help you through the next steps. This reflection can also help you recognize excuses or justifications during the behavior itself. You think your mother needs help with her grocery shopping and you can always meet this new person another time. Is your brain encouraging you to switch over to social media so that you can calm your mind and think better about the anxious task? Find your emotions and excuses during the reflection step.

Reason: You might enter this stage unknowingly from the last one. Think through the reflective thoughts and objectively ask yourself whether these justifications are valid. We can use the *first-things-first strategy* to comb through the excuses and see if they have any logic. Are they relevant to what you need right now? Do they make sense or are you buying time? Evaluate the negative self-talk in your mind. Pretend like you're the judge and jury and the reflective excuses are on trial.

Do you really think that postponing your task for social media is a good idea? Do you think it will make the task any easier or will it become more complicated because you're pressed for time? Think about your mother and question whether she went shopping alone before? Has she succeeded without you carrying her purse? Does she know where the store is and can she drive herself? The best way we can see if something is rational is to question every aspect of it until it makes sense to us.

Respond: Unfortunately, this is the highest breaking point for procrastinators because if they can't reason, they won't enter the right response stage. However, you *can* start replacing your thoughts and chosen actions before you proceed. The response step of the PURRRR protocol requires you to establish new actions based on the rationality of your reasoning. What steps can you take right now to change the procrastination urge?

Could you call your mom and make sure she has transport? Perhaps, you can send your blind date a message to confirm that you're on your way. You can also enlist a friend to keep you accountable by sending them a message. Tell them that you'll be with your date in an hour and they should check in with you.

You could also commit to changing your social media password and logging out. Use some crazy characters that you won't remember. You can always click on "forgot password" later. You want to provide your mind with alternatives that can cause procrastination to seem so much worse. Break the barriers down that protect the delay tactics. The idea in this step is to instruct yourself with new options guided with the *do it now* method. Finally, talk and walk yourself through the new actions you've chosen.

Revise: The final step helps us when we stray or when something hasn't gone as planned. Don't be hard on yourself if you fail to move from the reflection to the response stage productively. The truth is that this technique also requires practice. Also, you might reason with something that isn't rational. Anyone can make this wrongful decision. Remember that your loop doesn't shatter all at once. You'll find yourself frequently entering and adjusting the strategy to fit with your life and circumstances.

Think about the reasoning as the scope on your rifle and the chosen response is your aim. You might've missed and then you must reevaluate the strategy and look for new additions, alternatives, or rational thoughts. The reasoning is hardly perfect on the first few tries because your mind has been indoctrinated into thinking a certain way. This step often needs readjusting to perfect your PURRRR strategy.

No one knows everything and you can even collect new ideas and information when you missed the target the first time. A revision can also be used if you missed a step, such as forgetting the initial pause. Remember that active procrastinators are adaptable and they use the revision stage to strategize their intentional delays.

The PURRRR protocol will help you regain self-control with enough practice. Increased accuracy and faster timing will also come with time and your momentum will start snowballing. Let's summarize the technique.

Step 1: Pause by stopping your mind's inner dialogue for a moment.

Step 2: Utilize your resistance to be impulsive.

Step 3: Reflect and think about what's going on.

Step 4: Use your reasoning and logic to think things through.

Step 5: Respond by putting yourself through the reasonable paces you chose.

Step 6: Revise your strategy by making adjustments.

It will be challenging at first, but this process will become automatic until eventually your procrastination lessens. Be kind to yourself and don't aim for perfection! Progressive improvement is the best way to make this a new habit. Try to decrease your delay tactics by 10% and then another 10% and so on. Eventually, you'll have brought it down to a minimum and you can focus on using it actively.

Actionable Examples

You might be wondering how this process can be applied to any situation. I'm going to give you two examples to show you how it's been used in various styles of procrastination. There are no excuses immune to the powers of PURRRR.

Example One

Emma is a defier type of procrastinator and she has a long list of excuses why she needn't follow the rules. She has a new job writing for a newspaper, which she obtained through skills and experience. She didn't graduate from university because she couldn't sustain the deadlines. This places her in a predicament because writing comes with strict deadlines. She finds herself with the responsibility of finishing an article before it goes out to press tomorrow. Emma has the entire day and doesn't feel pressured to commit to it.

Unfortunately, the sun goes down and she gets a call from her best friend. Her friends are attending a movie premiere tonight and before she knows it, she's dressed for the event. She has put her article off the entire day and thinks she can rush it when she returns home. Emma can enact the pause immediately as she becomes aware of her intentions. The momentary pause gives you a silent state to think. She then shifts into the *utilize* stage to stop herself from applying make-up. Her mind and body become silent now.

Now she starts reflecting on the option she chose. She feels a little anxious about attending the premiere because she might be too tired to write when she gets back home. In fact, her friends will encourage her to go for a drink after, and this begins stirring more anxiety. Yes, she doesn't like following deadlines, but she may put her new job at risk if she doesn't finish her article tonight. It needs to be emailed to her editor before the newspaper goes to print.

Suddenly, she finds herself familiar and accepting of her genuine fears and has already subconsciously slipped into the next phase. She starts reasoning with the options before her. She can go to the premiere and face her boss tomorrow. It's a once in a lifetime opportunity after all. Besides, she could write a piece about the new movie. Her first option has potential and consequences. Now she reasons with another option. Staying home and completing her article will keep her job safe and she can show reliability for the first time in her life.

Workplace reliability can eventually lead to a promotion. It doesn't matter what Emma uses to reason both sides, as long as she finds the logic in both options. Besides, going to the premiere isn't relevant to her writing job, because she writes an advice column for new mothers. Is she going to advise new moms to go watch the apocalyptic movie? Perhaps, the moms can learn a few things about zombies who are somewhat similar to toddlers. Zombies have no impulse control after all. Logic seeps into her grasp. She understands both sides of the coin and can progress to the response stage. She talks herself through the steps and takes action.

She sends her friend a message to apologize for not making it to the premiere because she has an important deadline at work. This gives us a smooth example as Emma enters the revision stage during and after her actions to evaluate the decision. Her friend accepted her reason, which shows that Emma made the right choice. Besides, she's a defier. She doesn't need her friend's approval anyway. However, she delivers her article on time and finally feels proud. She also managed to write an impressive article through her experience about how new moms can be defiers, but they have to change their habits the moment they have a newborn baby to care for. Overall, her boss was impressed and complimented her. So, Emma experiences a reward and can catch up with her friends tonight to hear all about the movie.

Example Two

Let's complicate things now to help you understand how the PURRRR strategy can apply to difficult situations too. We'll use James and Mia for this example. James has been a variant procrastinator, much like my friend Richard. He's a crisis-maker, defier, and worrier, and like many other people, he suffers from multiple types of procrastination. This is when procrastinators often experience delayed actions in various parts of their lives. James has been a procrastinator of note; he met Mia a few months back and wants to take things further.

He has this whole evening planned to propose to Mia and ask her to move in. This is a huge step for 40-year-old James who has never been in a committed relationship. Deep down, he knows that he can't live without Mia. She informed him that she was offered a job in New York and would have to move soon. She has to decide by Monday. Now James plans this evening to ask her to stay. He knows that Mia is struggling to decide because you guessed it, she's also a procrastinator.

Besides, she's always lived on the west coast, and moving to New York is not an easy decision because she'll be away from all her friends and family. Mia thrives through her social life. However, our focus is on James for this example. It's Sunday and he's holding the phone in his hands, waiting to call Mia. He is nervous as hell and walks around his apartment with the phone in his hand. Before he realizes it, he puts the phone down and decides to watch a movie before he calls her.

James practices the PURRRR protocol and implements it as soon as he realizes what he's doing. He silences his mind, which is challenging because he is severely anxious. He quickly moves into utilization to stop himself from watching the movie and switches the television off. This gives him the peace and quiet he needs to reflect on how he feels right now. He is tearful because the woman he loves could be moving thousands of miles away. He has always delayed everything, but this isn't the time for that.

His emotions will be all over the place. Fear, anxiety, dread, and sadness are brewing inside of him. He starts reasoning with his options. He wonders if he should watch the movie now and stand a chance of losing contact when Mia gets too busy to answer her phone or if he should call her right now. He logically thinks of both benefits and consequences as he swiftly shifts into the response stage. His immediate response must be to call Mia before she can't be reached.

He'll be at work tomorrow and she'll be unavailable later as she always switches off on a Sunday afternoon. It's now or never for James! He jumps up and finds his phone before dialing Mia and nervously asking her to come over in the afternoon. Sadly, Mia has other plans and won't be home until late. James is crushed and his PURRRR didn't get his engine oiled. He shifts straight into the revision phase and devises a new plan. He will show up at her door tonight with flowers and a ring.

He won't let this go. He runs through the reflection, reason, and response paces again to plan his new venture. In a perfect world, James makes it and Mia says yes. James can revise his response once more to make sure he's consciously aware of the rewards that came from his decision.

Honestly, you can use the PURRRR protocol to help you through most situations because it's adaptable. If something doesn't work, try something else.

Chapter 8:

Goals and Rewards

You knew this was coming. Goals are the nemesis of procrastinators because they don't only struggle with keeping them, but they also struggle with choosing and starting them. It's understandable when we think of the habit loop and how hard it is to break it. Many procrastinators have set their eyes on the posts before, but they failed. The reason for this is that they try to set unreliable, unreachable, and impossible goals. The real truth is that you've achieved many goals in your life, but you fail to recognize them. This chapter will help you understand why I say that. It's the faceoff between outcome and behavioral goals that will cure your procrastination.

Mistakes and Corrections

Losing track of your ambitions is as easy as following directions from a French tourist in Japan. The mistake is that we understand goals as this long-term desire of who and what we want to be. We visualize the result without reading between the lines. Making it your life's mission to stop procrastination is an outcome goal. Being fit is another long-term goal. Being the best employee and marrying your soulmate before you hit 40 are both outcome goals. Keep in mind that this is particularly true for people who haven't even met their soulmate yet. Nevertheless, finishing your presentation for work is also an outcome goal.

Decorating your home, getting good grades in school, and breaking up with your romantic partner are all outcome goals. The list can go on to include losing weight, writing a book, or finishing a marathon. Are you starting to see the problem here? Our minds are focused on where we want to be at the end of our journey, but everything in-between is blurred. It's easy to see yourself in a higher position at work or engaged to the love of your life, but both ambitions are somewhat ambiguous. They aren't tangible or observable. It's true that we can't set goals unless we have an end in sight.

The problem is that when we focus on the end without all the fluff in the middle, we are far more likely to fail. We cannot control something if we don't know how to get there. We can lose track of our progress and become overwhelmed with the long strides we need to take. These goals are unrealistic and might not even be relevant to what you want. You look at yourself in the mirror and see a plump ball staring back at you. Suddenly, you set an instant goal that you must lose 20 pounds to look better. How will weight loss make you look better precisely?

Will your cheekbones be more noticeable or will your double chin disappear? Besides, losing 20 pounds is a great goal but what needs to be done to get there? Wishful thinking doesn't come with details. Will you go to the gym for half an hour every morning? Will you eat healthier? What is healthy eating? Outcome-based goals are insanely frustrating to procrastinators because they keep trying with no progress. Perfectionists are particularly enraged by their inability to accomplish silly goals. An implosion is inevitable among delayers. This is where we can correct previous attempts by adding behavioral goals to the outdated predecessor.

You don't want your outcome to vanish either, but you want the two to collide into a guaranteed method for you to reach the end. Procrastination is a habit, a behavior, so why do you think that anything but behavioral changes will decrease it?

The Golden Rules

Behavioral goals are a technique for you to set your eyes on a target and use the strategic and measurable direction to get there. Think of it as a mapping solution to the person asking the tourist for directions. You can take control once you know where you're going and how to get there. Behavioral goals don't focus solely on the target, but they also focus on the entire process of getting there. It doesn't matter how complicated or lengthy the process is. You'll still be able to follow it step-by-step. The only secret is to know what you want before you start.

You'll also learn soon enough that small wins count as much as the end itself. Someone who had a late night will resist getting out of bed when they need to. Their goal might be to get milk from the supermarket, but there are steps before this can be achieved. For example, this person can't get milk if they refuse to get out of bed. They've already achieved a small goal for the day when they get up. Behavioral goals are all about the actions we take along the route we choose.

There are rules we can follow when we set behavioral goals. Let's see how you can also set achievable ambitions from this day forward. Any goal you choose should follow these guidelines to have a much better chance of succeeding. Keep in mind that the goal-setting strategy won't work if one rule is followed and you forget the others.

Rule number 1: Any target you set must be *observable.* Thinking about doing something isn't behavioral because people must be able to see what you're doing. You must be able to see your actions. You should be able to take photos of each step. Your body must be moving in a direction that expresses forward momentum. Your goal must be trackable by yourself and others. Wishful thinking is a thing of the past.

Don't aim for "feeling less stressed about all the steps you need to take before you can see your doctor." That makes no tangible sense. Rather say that you'll call your doctor for an appointment. Visualize yourself picking up the phone and dialing the number. You might have to start with finding the number first if you don't have it saved, but you get it. Thinking about how something should be less threatening is a waste of time.

Rule number 2: Your goal must be *specific and concrete* in every detail. Imagine you're the person who must get milk from the store. Even though this is an action, it must be specified. Will you get milk from your gas station or will you proceed to the mall? Being specific can be useful and prevent you from overlooking important details. You must be able to visualize precisely how your body will be moving during the steps you set. The first rule of observable never goes out of fashion.

Going to the mall requires you to brush your hair for example. Never think in vague terms and conditions when you set your goals. Having an idea of what you want to achieve in measurable terms is better than thinking about why you should get up today. This is how you facilitate getting the milk. This can work for any goal.

You might have procrastinated on cleaning your house for weeks now. Don't let this get you down and don't you dare say that you'll deal with it on Saturday. You know that you want to clean your house, but you won't do it unless you're specific. The thought will overwhelm you because you see yourself spending the entire day sweating like a beast. Rather make your intentions specific and say that you'll spend two hours cleaning the house on Saturday. Any progress is always better than none.

Rule number 3: You must be able to break your goal into *mini-goals* or *manageable steps.* Each mini-goal must also follow the rules. You should be able to observe and be specific with each step you take. Let's say that getting milk is the outcome goal. Getting out of bed is a challenging task when you spent the night out with friends. We're going to focus on the shorter goal here. You need milk for breakfast and coffee. This will get you started for the day. The first step you'll take is getting out of bed.

Your foot hitting the ground and your backside leaving the mattress is the first goal. Hopefully, you turn brushing your teeth and hair into another step if you're going to the mall. Choosing your clothes is another step and so is finding your car keys. The beauty of breaking our goals into specific steps is that it seems more vivid and simpler than a distant goal. That's why you're likely to achieve them.

The steps you set are also flexible if you realize that you forgot to add shoes to your list. I'm sure you'll be a smash hit at the mall with your slippers. These steps can also change according to the circumstances without you feeling guilty. You arrive at the mall, dolled up with make-up and your prettiest dress, but they're still closed. No worries, you can adaptably proceed to the gas station.

Rule number 5: You must be able to complete the *first step within two minutes.* James Clear who wrote the book *Atomic Habits*, a New York Times bestseller, can help us understand the value of two minutes (Clear, n.d.). Procrastinators are endlessly looking for the easy way out. Keeping your first step within the two-minute marker will decrease the chances of failure. It's so much easier to read one page of a book than it is to read an entire chapter.

It's much easier to give yourself two minutes to get out of bed than it is to focus on the drive to the store. We can rather concentrate on starting with folding one shirt that takes less than two minutes instead of looking at the pile of laundry laying on the couch. This rule reminds us to choose any action that requires minimal efforts as our first go. It also exercises our momentum as we start every goal with easy tasks. Clear explains that we must standardize before we can optimize new habits.

It doesn't matter too much that we struggle during this step, but we're exercising the momentum and motivation aspects gradually. This can also help people who face challenging studies. A teenager will be paralyzed by fear before an exam, but they'll calm down once they pass those two minutes.

Rule number 5: Keep a *time limit* on all mini-goals. Any goal that has no time-restraints is likely to fail. You've already met a milestone if you tell yourself that you have two minutes to get out of bed. A writer will give themselves an hour to conjure up 200 words. They'll be proud of themselves for reaching those words and possibly more when the hour is over. This rule helps us track and measure our progress.

The moment you see your hair looking normal and you're dressed for the mall is the moment you realize that you've accomplished something already. The same applies to someone who chooses to spend two hours cleaning on Saturday. They've officially reached their goal if they do it. Give yourself reasonable due dates for your tasks.

Rule number 6: We need to be *realistic* about our goals to ensure success. Procrastinators think in terms of ideal situations, forgetting that they're only human and have limited time and energy. Don't promise yourself that you'll be awarded employee of the month unless you're capable of reaching this. Besides, that goal fails all the other rules anyway. You also shouldn't demand that you pass your exams tomorrow or design a complex presentation when you don't even know what PowerPoint is.

The first one can't be achieved unless you have time and energy to study. The second one can't be achieved unless you have time and energy to gain the skills needed and design the slideshow. You're only human, no matter what you think. The realistic rule can be added by setting a *minimum acceptable goal.* Make a concerted effort to find one that is relevant to the outcome goal and keeps your skills, time, and energy in mind.

What is the smallest goal you can set that would help you feel accomplished and proud? This is necessary for the reward that comes after reaching it. *Minimal steps* will stop you from being overwhelmed and you can rather focus on painting one room in the house today instead of painting the entire outside. Don't set yourself up for failure by killing your motivation unintentionally.

Rule number 7: How can we forget about the *rewards* that will eventually set the tone for new habits in our goal system? Procrastinators are experts when it comes to beating themselves up for simple mistakes, but they don't know how to be kind to themselves. They fail to see progress even when they genuinely deserve recognition. Rewards seal the new loop you're creating and it drives your motivation, passion, and new habits. Choose a milestone you can reach and reward.

Even travelers need to stop and stock up on energy and food. Think of your rewards as your pitstop along the way. You've learned to apply measurable steps, so now you can reward progress. The only condition here is to keep it relevant to your progress. Don't book a weekend trip for getting out of bed. Decided milestones can be rewarded with what you can afford and enjoy.

This could be a weekend trip for a larger milestone. You can also go to the movies, visit your favorite restaurant, get coffee with a friend, or read a book. You must enjoy the reward. That's what should be relevant here. Rewards establish positive reinforcement that increases your likelihood of continuing the new behavior.

Rule number 8: You need to *assess your progress weekly*. This allows you to notice the progress you've made or the lack of it. Procrastinators never accept and acknowledge their small steps along the way. Keep a diary and record your progress which is then assessed. Look at how much you've done to get this far. You might've taken steps that weren't even part of your original plans. They moved you forward anyway and this means that they count.

Don't overlook the tiny steps either. Give yourself credit because getting out of bed counts. Switching your laptop on also counts. Making that call to the doctor's office counts. Use the assessment to revise your plans if you didn't reach a goal. You'll see where you went off track and can change this next week. The goal might not have been important to you and that's why you missed the deadline. Perhaps, it doesn't align itself with your values and priorities.

It might be so far from your interests that it lacks passion. The assessment could also reveal a lack of structure or following the rules. The missed target might have fallen short of actionable steps. Reevaluate the outcome you have in mind to resolve this issue. Then you can work through mapping the route again.

Chapter 9:

Goals and Rewards Part Two: The Trial

The best way for you to approach behavioral goal setting is to give it a try. This exercise chapter is going to help you experiment with your new goal-setting system for one week. I want you to commit to a week of trying it out. All you have to do is make an effort to have a growth mindset. You must adopt an attitude of learning. This can be from success or failure. I encourage you to prepare an openness for a challenge. Keep in mind that even a failure is only a learning curve and this isn't an examination of your wits, talents, intellect, or responsibility.

No one is watching you after all. In fact, you're most welcome to do this experiment with one of your support people. Someone can hold you accountable or make it seem less challenging by doing this with you. Think of yourself as a researcher for this exercise. You can keep a diary to record things as you go along. You also want a sheet that can remind you of the next step. Forgetfulness can happen and it will make you feel worse. The sheet can prevent forgetfulness. Go through the steps and find your way through this week. It won't be as hard as you think.

Preparation

The first step you take when planning your week is choosing your goal. Ask yourself what you'd like to achieve in the next week. What time frames will you give each step of the goal? Keep the rules in mind at all times. Your goal should be able to break up into mini-goals, be specific, and observable. So, you're choosing a specific outcome goal that you can turn into a behavioral goal. Make notes of various ambitions you have this week. They don't need to be your life's ultimate goal.

It can be to eat healthier, finish a book, or go on a date. You can narrow it down to the winning option once you have all your notes. You're only choosing one goal in this exercise. This is unheard of for procrastinators, but having only one goal will remove aversiveness and help you work towards it without too much traction. Procrastinators often take on more than they can handle, so you also remove this possibility. I'm going to choose an ambitious, fictional goal for the first example.

The Roommate Conundrum

I have a spare bedroom that's been my hoarder cave for years now. I store all my excess stuff in there and I've needed to clear it out for a while. I need to find a roommate to share my living costs with and can't do this until I start clearing the room out. That sets the stage for my goal. I know what I want to work towards. I'm bravely giving myself one week to do it. That's step one.

The preparation stage might seem rather daunting. It doesn't define the details, but that's what the schedule is for. Bring your sheet forth and start planning your goal without ever forgetting the rules you've learned about. I'm going to start by splitting my week into more manageable segments. I have seven days to make a dent in the boxes and rubble stored in the room. I shall now allocate time for one hour every morning and for one hour every evening. This gives me 14 hours over the week to make progress. Also, these mini-schedules aren't that threatening because I'm confident I can stay focused or one hour at a time.

However, these are larger goals and might not be for you. This is only an example though. I cannot forget the two-minute rule either, but I'll get there. My outcome goal is 14 hours spread over the week. I must also break the hour session down. What's the first thing I'll do within the two minutes to get started? I'll walk inside the room and choose one box to sort through.

This box will be placed on top of the study desk and opened. That's it for my two-minute rule. If I get past the rule, which is highly probable once I've caught a glimpse of what's inside the box, my stepping schedule continues.

Next, I must dedicate another five minutes at a time. I want to remove 10 items from the box within the first five minutes. These items will go into a goodwill or paperwork box I've placed on the floor. I must keep my paperwork to sort because throwing it out without sorting through it can create problems. The only rule here in the first week is that you're not allowed to read anything unless it's in the allocated time that you set for paperwork. Reading these papers in other behavioral slots will only delay and distract you.

Let's see how my one-week experiment could look on paper. I'm going to be slightly vague for the purposes of my example, but your version should be more detailed than this.

Monday morning: I have two minutes to choose and open the first box. I'd like to sort five boxes out this morning.

Monday evening: I shall stick to my two-minute promise and choose my next "first box." I must sort out four more boxes this evening and move the filled goodwill boxes to my car.

Tuesday morning: Place my morning coffee on the sorting study desk to make myself start my day there.

Sort through another two boxes and fill another goodwill box. Take this to the car, get into the car, and leave the house five minutes earlier than usual. Drop the boxes at goodwill on my way to work.

Tuesday evening: I'm going to dedicate this slot to my paperwork. I won't do this in the room itself. I'll move to the dining table and sort the few papers I've found into a trash and filing pile. Throw away the trash paperwork.

Wednesday morning: Start with one box and then another three. Move the empty boxes to the garbage bin.

Wednesday evening: Stop at the stationery store to collect new files for the paperwork I sorted last night. Put the paperwork in the right files when I arrive home. Remove my socks from the drawer and add them to another one before I store the newly sorted files there.

Thursday morning: Open all the drawers on the left of the study desk within two minutes. Sort the trash out and take it to the garbage bin.

Thursday evening: Open all the right-hand side drawers and sort the trash out. Dispose of this and put all stationery and useful goodies into a small container. Add any paperwork to your final sorting pile.

Friday morning: Put the new paperwork on the breakfast table and sort them into piles while eating breakfast. Move the papers to their appropriate files and leave home five-minutes early with the last of the goodwill boxes. Drop this box off on the way to work.

Friday evening: Use my two minutes to ask my boss if I can leave earlier today so that I can stop by a second-hand shop on the way home. Ask the dealer to visit me tomorrow morning and leave my contact details. Give them a time that suits my morning hour. Stop at the supermarket on the way home to purchase cleaning products.

Saturday morning: My biggest challenge will be to let the second-hand dealer into my apartment and take them through to the bedroom. This will consume two minutes. My target is to have them purchase as much of the unnecessary furniture in the room, if not everything. I'll need to negotiate with them to also trade for a bed which they must deliver on Sunday morning.

Saturday afternoon: Place all the cleaning agents in sight as my two-minute motivator. Vacuum the floor and wipe the walls down. Clean the spiderwebs out of the corners and open the windows for fresh air.

Sunday morning: My negotiated bed should arrive if all goes well. Opening the door for them on a Sunday morning counts as my two minutes. I'll help the movers place the bed and the bedside cabinets in the room. The cleaning products are still in the room to wipe the new furniture down.

Sunday afternoon: My two minute-start is to take a photo of the bedroom. Switch my computer on and upload the photo to my preferred advertising platform. Design an advert with words that describe the look and feel of the room. Remember to mention my preferences when it comes to gender and hygiene habits. Choose a weekly or monthly rental and make the advert go live.

Do you see how simple the hour applications are? I manage to list my spare bedroom by the end of the week if all goes as planned.

Look at the sheet you've planned and make sure it's doable. You don't want to overwhelm yourself either. Don't give yourself four hours total to finish a huge task. I've chosen a larger goal here but it was simple to break it up as needed. My many mini-goals have made the week's schedule realistic. You must have viable steps for each session you plan. Mine remains slightly vague in that sense. Your schedule should contain the two-minute step to start every session. This can be opening the drawer, lifting a box, switching the laptop on, or placing your morning coffee where you need to start.

It doesn't matter how small the step is, as long as it's moving you towards your goal. The night I choose to place the goodwill box in my car is already setting the stage for the next morning. I also left my cleaning products in the room until I was done with them. Assess your chosen schedule and don't be afraid to make reasonable alterations during the week if you get stuck. I could've hit a brick wall if the second-hand dealer never showed up. We can't control something like that, but we can make sure our first step on Saturday morning is to pick the phone up and call them as a reminder.

Finally, it's a great idea to get some feedback on your schedule. Call that friend who can hold you accountable or the one who's doing this experiment with you and ask them to give you feedback. They might see that your goal is too unrealistic.

Self-Improvement

The next example will require all the same rules and processes as the first. Sally has an opportunity to broaden her horizons at work with a promotion. However, she doesn't have the skills required. She loosely understands the position, but she doesn't have the paperwork needed by her company. Sally has been a receptionist at the company for 20 years. Her older colleague retired and a human resources position has opened. Before Sally can work on her schedule as I did with the roommate idea, she needs to understand exactly what she wants first.

Her outcome goal is to apply for the new position. Now she must turn this into a behavioral goal. Let's see how she can plan her week assuming that she received the news on Thursday afternoon.

Thursday afternoon: Sally will have to approach her boss or the retiring colleague to find out more about the role. Stepping into the office is the first step for her. Striking up a conversation can also be within the two-minute rule. Sally asks her colleague what's needed for the position and what she can do to get there. The fact that Sally has been with the company for 20 years shows that she's reliable, so they might consider her if she can show some promise. Her colleague will give her an idea of what's needed and this is the only thing Sally needs to do today.

Friday morning: Sally has had the night to think things through and prepare for her week ahead. All she needs to do when she arrives at work is to let her colleague or boss know that she's interested and will present them with an application next Thursday.

Friday evening: Sally can give herself another 15 minutes in the evening to research what she can do to be suitable for the application. Switching her laptop on and hitting enter on the Google search bar are her two-minutes done. She must find three options for making herself suitable. She can diarize the contact details of the night classes available. Keep in mind that Sally could rely on being a licensed coach because she already knows and understands everyone at work. She needn't spend months at university.

Saturday morning: Sally decides to make it her mini-goals to call the colleges to find out about times, prices, and qualifications. She has her notepad ready and picking up the phone is the first step. Dialing the number and speaking to the person on the other end is another step. These calls don't need to be long and dreary either. She can simply ask for the details to be emailed to her. This entire session shouldn't cost Sally more than half an hour.

Sunday morning: Sally's first step is to switch her laptop on and open her emails in two minutes. She can spend 20 minutes reading the material each person sent her and then she can switch off for the weekend. Sally will subconsciously be thinking about what she read and wouldn't need to decide today.

Monday morning: Sally has a good idea of which course will help her. She also knows that she has time and energy for it, as well as being able to afford it. She should give it some serious thought for 10 more minutes. She decides to spend this time developing a pros and cons list. Reaching for the paper and pen is the first step here. Now she has weighed the pros and cons of each college and can keep her list close by for reference.

Tuesday morning: Sally's advantages and disadvantages have been thought through for more than 24 hours and she can commit to deciding this morning. She must open her emails and respond to the college she chooses. All she needs to do today is to fill out her information and send it back.

Wednesday morning: Sally will dedicate her morning break at work to call the college and confirm their receipt where she signed up for the classes. The hardest part again is picking up the phone. It's also essential for her to ask them to send over proof of her upcoming classes. She can receive this via email and print it out at work.

Thursday morning: It's Sally's final day and she promised to hand in her application. However, her journey today starts by opening her emails and printing the documents that the college sent over. Now she can fill in the application for the human resources position and attach her college papers. The last thing she needs to do is hand it over.

Please note that Sally's example is very simple, but I wanted to share one complex and one simple example of the one week trial. Both are still pretty vague, but some details are highly specific. Sally needs to open her emails before she can start. I need to log into my advertising website before I can list my apartment. Small steps should be rife in your plan for the week. Both of these examples are a job well done if you complete them. I could spoil myself with a mountain hike or Sally can have dinner with friends on Friday to celebrate her accomplishment.

Chapter 10:

Motivation and Self-Control

The last two chapters have taught you how to set goals, strive for progress, and be specific and realistic. However, you haven't learned much about the motivation and self-control you'll need to adopt for optimal results. You make a promise to yourself as soon as you prepare a schedule for the trial week. You don't want to break this promise, do you? Delivery is possible with the final addition to goal-setting the proper way. The tips in this chapter will keep you focused on motivation and commit you to make positive changes.

The Motivation Spectrum

Before we can get you motivated to achieve the goals you've set, we must teach you where your motivation can slip. Knowing where your shortfalls lie can help you overcome them with simple strategies. The most common reason we lack motivation is when our ability, agency, values, or interest falls short. You won't be motivated to do something you don't have the abilities or skills to complete. You struggle to reach for goals when your agency or sense of control is gone. Every person wants to be in control and the less we have, the lower our motivation sinks. Also, if we don't value the completion of a task or the achievement of a goal, we won't be motivated. Keep in mind that interests and values are different things.

You might value the concept or importance of something even if you have no interest in it. Sam values his ability to maintain fitness, but he doesn't love it. He knows that it's important to lead a healthy life and that's what motivates him. Interest is when Sam loves what he does. He spends hours at the gym and focuses on everything he eats. A lack of interest in a goal could also set you off track. These four deterrents are the most common reasons we feel demotivated. They can stem from anxiety, fear of failure, lack of knowledge, or a lack of purpose in life. On the other end of the spectrum, we learn to understand what can motivate us.

Two kinds of motivation can either drive us or shut us down interchangeably. Intrinsic motivation is internal, and it involves our thoughts, beliefs, values, emotions, and self-satisfaction. The most important and attainable goals in your life will come from internal motivation. Our values are the rules by which we live: we learned them in our childhood and they direct our thoughts and beliefs. Your idea of right and wrong is your values, but everyone prioritizes them differently. Many of your justifications are influenced by values and beliefs. Clarifying your values could boost your motivation if they align themselves with your goals.

A sense of purpose is another powerful motivator. Every person wants and has a purpose in life, whether they realize it or not. A purpose defines what you wish to contribute to the world and not just yourself. A mom thinks that her purpose is to feed and school her child, but she also has a greater duty to him. She must be the example who teaches her child to contribute to the world when his time comes. Our purpose can help determine where we see ourselves in the future.

Extrinsic motivation is when we reach for a goal to achieve a better reputation, higher salary, or to gain approval from other people. Intrinsic motivators are driven by their purpose for self-gratification, whereas extrinsic motivators are driven by other people's approval of us. Higher salaries make us feel great inside, but they are a reflection of someone's opinion of us. You can't control your extrinsic motivation because it relies on other people, but you can control your intrinsic motivation and get the ball rolling.

Breaking Through the Wall

You must find strategies that work for you to overcome the motivation blockers. There are various options you can try. Test them out as you're working through your week-long experiment. Let's understand each one to give you a push in the right direction.

What Excuses?

One way to break through is to recognize your excuses. An excuse is merely a crossroads in the pathway of doing it and avoiding it. It's not an action and it's not a definitive route either. Excuses bring you to a decision, and all you need to do is choose the right path. You can either procrastinate or you can work your way through it, five minutes at a time. You've learned about your most common excuses in an earlier chapter. You can also work on solving these.

Don't allow yourself to delay instantaneously. You can choose the progressive path and even transform the excuse into a motivation driver. Think about your excuse and listen to what it's telling you. "I feel like surfing now, so I can do this later." This one is simple because it can change to: "I'll get 15 minutes of work done now and then reward myself with a short stroll on the beach." This is called flipping the motivation switch.

You've suddenly halted your loop into recognizing that work can lead to an interesting reward. Sally from the previous chapter could be telling herself: "I can take the weekend off and think about my college options next week." This doesn't seem dangerous but it is. She can flip this back into her schedule by saying: "I'll spend 10 minutes looking through the options today and have the remainder of the day to think about them calmly."

Setting the Scene

Distractions are a procrastinator's worst nightmare. Chances are that they offer you more internal motivation because you have a keen interest in them. Netflix just reminded you about a new season of your favorite show. Now you're struggling to stay motivated and control your impulses. The best thing to do is to change your Netflix password to something ridiculous and recover it when you're done.

Switch off your phone, television, and anything else that makes a noise to distract you. This includes switching off from chatty friends when you have an exam tomorrow or you need to focus. The fact that you're setting short spurts of progress is the reason why you need all of your focus. Your environment should be clear of people and devices that tempt you to stray.

Reframe

Psychologist Alicia Clark explains that we can turn our negative internal dialogue into a positive force if we allow it (Clark, n.d.). Your internal dialogue will remind you of the time you failed and bring awful memories into your sphere. It will talk you down and instruct you to think of tasks negatively. However, you can speak to your internal dialogue. I don't necessarily mean that you must talk to yourself in the middle of a park. It can also be an internal discussion. You can force new thoughts into your mind by doing this. You can also say them out loud if you're alone.

Some people call these mantras but we call them a conversation with our internal critic. Stand in front of the mirror and repeat positive affirmations to yourself. Your mind will resist and this is when you close your eyes and envision yourself reaching your goals. Become entwined with the emotions that rush through your body as you watch yourself succeed mentally. Force a smile if you can. Tell yourself that you choose to do this and push the "have to do this" idea into oncoming traffic.

This motivation breaker can help us turn our thoughts and emotions positive. It might take some practice, but you know that by now. The main thing is that you must force positive thoughts into your mind. Visualization remains a powerful force when you close your eyes and walk through the paces of your goal. Welcome all the feelings as you do this. Allow the internal changes to shift your motivation into gear. Go through every step you'll take, even if it's picking up the phone.

Visualization doesn't only motivate us. It can also help us prepare mentally. It becomes easier to cross the threshold between thinking and doing when you've practiced it in your mind. Exposing yourself to the negative thoughts and feelings before you start on the goal is key to taking the fear out of the experience. It doesn't mean you'll suddenly be fearless, but you'll notice that it dissipates. This will shut down the negative talk in your mind.

Key Notes

Remove the fear of failure by aiming lower. This sounds negative, but your expectations can get in the way of your motivation too. You've learned that motivation can be blocked by a sense of not knowing enough or not being able to do it in time. Your mini-goals must focus on achieving completion rather than perfection. Getting something done is better than not doing it at all.

Flexibility is also key. Allow for stumbles along the way because you'll continue tripping if you dwell on them. Take the person looking for a roommate. What if the second-hand dealer never brought the bed on time? That doesn't matter because they still list the bedroom unfurnished until they get a bed. We must be flexible as strict goals can harm our motivation too.

Commitment is the third cornerstone of any mini-goal. Keep the *do it now strategy* at heart and commit yourself. You can remove the blocker from this goal if you feel that the accomplishment doesn't fit into your internal motivation. Why doesn't it fit? Are you lacking the skills you need? Do you feel out of control? Commitment can also be driven by purpose. Remind yourself why you've chosen this task and what it adds to your overall contribution.

How to Master Self-Discipline and Commitment

Not every strategy will work for each person. There are a few more rabbits in the hat because self-discipline doesn't happen overnight.

Prioritize and Optimize

Optimizing your schedule can make things easier, and motivate you to carry on. Know the difference between urgent and important goals by learning about Eisenhower's principle (Mind Tools Content Team, n.d.). Important activities focus on intrinsic motivation, whereas urgent activities focus on extrinsic motivation. Eisenhower's principle teaches us that we must optimize our goal pursuit by combining urgent and important tasks. This way, we focus our efforts on internal and external motivation at the same time, giving the goal a double whammy effort.

Where you plan to begin can be crucial to your success, as so can when you choose to start. Go through your intended mini-goals for the week and determine which are priorities. Which goals can tick both boxes at the same time? This will help you plan better and you can combat the more stressful choices earlier in the day. Prioritize everything, such as waking up, dressing for work, eating breakfast, driving to work, and hosting a boardroom presentation. You'll become the master of your schedule in no time and this prevents a lack of motivation.

It also helps you commit to your schedule. Commitment is relative and will depend on your strategic motivation. You'll have more time and energy to knock the stressful tasks out first. Think about how Sally focused on her college tasks in the mornings before she was flustered. The roommate-seeker was even filing papers while having breakfast. This is part of optimization, as crazy as it seems. However, this doesn't give you an excuse to take on multitasking if this is your weakness.

The environment is the other part of optimization. You can't study for an exam if your friends are distracting you. Some fail at their projects because they choose bustling coffee shops to work instead of the controlled environment at home. Think about every factor that plays a role here. Commitment can also be obtained by calling your accountability partner to keep tabs on you. Let them check in with you at given times. Finally, mastering your plans will help you become an active procrastinator in time.

Timely Discipline

Time limits are the saviors of your sanity. Becoming a master planner will help you but you also need to stick to the time slots. Lengthy goals, activities, and tasks will make you lose interest. The more amped you are by the anxiety around the task, the deadline, and values tied to it, the more you'll experience internal motivation (Clark, n.d.). Anxiety can also increase your motivation, but you won't gain natural momentum if you set these ridiculous time slots. Stick to shorter time limits for each task so that it's easier to begin.

Many people go overboard as well. The secret here is that you must know when to stop. You've planned to work on a project for half an hour today. Set a timer and stop when your alarm rings. Don't extend your task because your motivation is snowballing or your interests have been stirred. This can actually backfire when you realize that you failed to complete the task you set out after that one.

It doesn't matter if you're feeling inspired or productive and think you won't be tomorrow. Missing other responsibilities will only send you into a downward stress spiral. The truth is that being productive today and expecting the same tomorrow is a fallacy. We prevent this fallacy by opening our eyes and sticking to the time we chose on the schedule. You have a bracket and that's where you'll stay. Make another promise to yourself to stay within the bracket.

One at a Time

Another method of honing your self-discipline is to devote all your attention to one task at a time. Don't worry about the next one because this removes effort from the current one. You'll feel a sense of accomplishment if you do a task well, especially if you didn't expect it. Be present with everything you do, from brushing your hair to designing a new logo for a client. You shut down any chances of distractions penetrating your schedule at incorrect times by doing this too. On the other hand, this discipline will prevent you from giving in to the urge to multitask when you shouldn't.

Stop thinking that you must do everything yourself because you know this leads to failure. Overdoers will fall into the trap of messing one project up because they focused on too many simultaneously. Get help when you need it. You can hire a cleaner to take care of the house while you're having a tough week at work. Outsource your duties, well, those that aren't internal. You can't ask a cleaner to work on a video for your friend's wedding while you clean up. Outsource the right way so that you can focus on the correct task.

Working Around Obstacles

There are two matters we haven't covered in this book. They shouldn't be part of your routine but they'll show up when you least expect it. The obstacles we must master to become self-disciplined are controlling our energy and boredom levels. We haven't even covered boredom in the book, but that's because it's as much an acceptable definition of procrastination as laziness is. These are two excuses that often interfere with our commitments and discipline.

Secret number 1: Energy comes from a healthy lifestyle. This is a scary thought for procrastinators but the best way to defeat this enemy is to live healthily. Start eating healthier, exercising, and check with your doctor if your hormone levels are right. Hormones can trick us into believing that we need sleep or food when we don't. I recommend that you speak to your doctor about subtle changes. Healthy lifestyles are an entire book on their own. Convincing a procrastinator to get healthy is like asking a tree to move so you can get sun. Only you can do this but I want you to be aware that it can impact your mastery if you ignore it.

Secret number 2: Boredom is an easily dismissed symptom of delay tactics. It can certainly throw a spanner in your hard work to stick to your commitment. Boredom makes us look for distractions. It's disguised under a low-level of anxiety or disinterest. The only way to defeat boredom is to ignore it and commit to the goal you choose. It's only a passing feeling and can't control you, so don't allow it to.

Bonus Chapter 11:

The Freedom From Procrastination Code

Changing our mindset to a positive one is a daily ritual we must repeat. We can do this with *the freedom from procrastination code*. You can either stand in front of the mirror each morning and repeat these mantras to yourself before you start the day, or you can implement appropriate mantras when you find yourself entering the procrastination spiral. Be assertive in your tone of voice and believe in what you're saying for this to work. Positive mantras could stop procrastination dead in its tracks when you confront your inner dialogue. Turning this into a daily routine will help them sink into your subconscious mind. You can also develop a few of your own when you recognize where you need positive influence over your inner dialogue.

Exercise Your Vocal Cords

Refer to this list in the morning or when you feel overwhelmed and want to postpone a task. Feel free to be as loud as you can when you're alone. You can even do this in the car on the way to work. Other drivers will simply think that you're singing along to music on your car radio.

Perfection is a myth, and I accept that it isn't possible.

An effort isn't a sign of weakness or stupidity, but rather a show of perseverance and resilience.

I don't fear failure because it's an ordinary part of life. Fear of failure is simply a doorway standing between me and living my best life.

I'm only human, everyone is only human, and we all have limitations.

The words challenge and adversity are opportunities to learn in disguise.

Anything worth doing is deserving of a few teachable mistakes along the way.

I deserve success just as much as the next person, and I'll handle all the inevitable reactions from others.

Doing well or not this time will still mean that I have choices next time.

I still retain power over my decisions even when I choose to follow someone else's rules.

Showing the real me will make sure I have real relationships, with genuine people who love me as I am.

There are always options, but it's up to me to find one that's right for me.

I have a bottomless well of courage and confidence if I choose to use it.

I am more than I allow myself to be. I can do what I set my mind to and accomplish what needs to be done.

I am focused and attentive to my goal in this present moment.

I'll observe my promised progress today so that I can acknowledge my strides.

I am the master of my attention and focus.

Negativity isn't part of my vocabulary; I can only say productivity.

I am worthy of the achievements that come from commitment.

I am no longer a slave to my mind and I instruct it now.

My focus brings a new calmness.

I have the power to face difficult situations with courage, grace, and effort.

I have an abundance of capabilities to find solutions.

Life is not a challenge, but rather an adventure waiting for me to take the plunge.

I will take one step closer to achieving the goal I've chosen in the next two minutes.

Resistance is futile and has no power over me anymore.

I can see the outcome and I've chosen the actions to get there.

I refuse to succumb to doubt, guilt, fear, or pessimism anymore.

I can visualize the steps I must take to reach my ambitions.

I have a renewed strength to move through, over, and under any obstacles in my way.

Planning and committing to my goals will give me a sense of deserved pride when I reach my heart's desire.

Each small goal brings me one step closer to the larger picture.

My mind lives happily in the present and doesn't wander off into timelines that don't exist anymore or yet.

I look forward to exploring new adventures, tasks, relationships, and decisions.

Conclusion

Theodore Roosevelt once said: "In a moment of decision, the best thing you can do is the right thing to do, the next best thing is the wrong thing, and the worst thing you can do is nothing." Procrastination has been your friend when it should've been a foe. It's much easier to do nothing when we aren't sure of ourselves or the task ahead of us. It's the easy way out and often comes with some misunderstood relief, however temporary it might be. I must finish my project for work before Monday, but I'm so entwined in the activity I'm busy with now. Who wants to leave an adventure with their friends when they have work to do?

Weighing the fun with the practicality of work is hard on most people. I would hate to leave a music festival early because I have a deadline. The laughter, music, and dance are tempting beyond pleasing my boss. I'd be glued to social media feeds about it even when I finally manage to tear myself away from the festival. I want to see what my friends are doing. I must read every update and watch every video as my work files lie beside the laptop screen that's glimmering with excitement.

In another example, who doesn't wish to avoid an awkward conversation with their family because the time isn't right? The time is never right anyway. It doesn't matter how we continue to suffer in silence as our happiness slips. I want to tell my mom that I'm raising my children without the harsh punishments I grew up with. We don't live in the dark ages of physical discipline anymore. However, I better put it off until another time because everyone's enjoying Thanksgiving dinner too much. It will simply cause tension. The problem is that the next time she threatens my toddler with a smack I'll probably explode. Then I've postponed the assertive and reasonable conversation we could've had instead, and replaced it with a holiday argument. The consequences are when a scene breaks out and I can't raise my child without negativity anymore. How am I an example when I'm aggressively telling my mom to shut up, but I want my child to have manners? Kids learn from watching their parents and family members after all.

Procrastinators are also notorious for staying in unhealthy relationships because there is too much effort and emotion involved in breaking it off. Maybe your romantic partner has been working on your last nerve. They continue to belittle you in front of your friends and family, and your friends don't even want to be around the awkwardness anymore.

All you've done so far is complain to them. You've delayed the inevitable break-up where you tell the person to hit the road, and in doing so, you've delayed your happiness and mental wellbeing. How long are your friends going to stick around to see you being belittled at every social event?

You might've delayed an important responsibility at work. All you had to do was call the repairman and print a notice for the coffee maker. Now, Amy has plugged it back in and electrocuted herself. Procrastination always leads to consequences where you must often pay for financial damages. You'll have to find the money to cover Amy's medical bills.

Let's not forget that you could lose your job for failing to follow simple instructions. Perhaps, you've been delaying some repair work at home too. You were supposed to pay someone to repair the garbage disposal. Now you have to wash your dishes in the bathtub while you wait for the repairman to show up.

There are endless examples and consequences that come from them. Some consequences are mild, whereas others will change your life drastically. Someone who fails to file their taxes on time can get into legal trouble. Failing to pay your phone bill can cause you to be disconnected and you won't be able to communicate with your clients.

I've shown you how the internal consequences can lead you straight into the clutches of anxiety, chronic stress, and insecurities. You've also learned about the external consequences which you might've already experienced. I think you've suffered from some consequences of your procrastination habits, or you wouldn't have read this book. It doesn't matter how severe or mild these consequences are because they can build up into a huge life change. You can lose your home, job, and spouse. Friends can ignore you and family can block your number. Procrastination stands between you and success. It also blocks your growth at work, home, and even in your hobbies.

This book has given you the tools to find out where you went astray. It has also taught you how to identify the obstacles and automatic mindsets you have. Awareness is a key element to progress. We can't improve something we refuse to admit. You might've tried other tools before but you quickly realized that people focus on the problem rather than the solution; that's the worst type of advice for a procrastinator. You weren't looking for approval and confirmation of all the questions. You needed answers and definitive steps to take.

I've given you the facts about what happens in your brain when you delay projects and situations, but I've stuck to the basics without overwhelming your mind with irrelevant information. Procrastination is a subconscious process that happens beneath most people's comprehension. You can correct it once you understand what actually happens. You have what it takes as long as you learn about the practical, proven methods of reaching the other side. Your brain must be taught how to change. You have control of your life and simple techniques can get you there. Besides, you can always rely on the fast-acting tools you have now when you find yourself straying from your goals. Ambitions are necessary for life, but we must understand how to master them.

You'll become the master of your own life as long as you practice the exercises in this book. Everyone is different, but we all want happiness, success, and progress. This toolkit has given you the means to achieve this. Some people will worry about their motivation and that's a valid argument. However, there are ways of getting around it and you know how to do this now. You won't only make progress with step-by-step momentum, but you'll also learn to enhance your end results.

I've used the techniques in this book to improve my own life and I'm confident that their simplicity will give you the push you need. Be the best version of yourself, the one that will astonish other people and allow you the pride you deserve. All you need to do is stick to the plan you have now.

References

30 Goal Setting Affirmations to Stop Your Procrastination. (2020, June 9). Develop Good Habits. www.developgoodhabits.com/goal-affirmations-stop-procrastinating/

Burka, J. B. & Yuen, L. M. (2008). *Procrastination: Why You Do It, What to Do About It.*

Cherry, K. & Susman, D. (2020, May 30). *What is procrastination?* Very Well Mind. www.verywellmind.com/the-psychology-of-procrastination-2795944

Clark, A. H. (n.d.). *Stop procrastination and eliminate anxiety – Here's how.* Find a Psychologist. www.findapsychologist.org/stop-procrastination-and-eliminate-anxiety-heres-how-by-dr-alicia-h-clark/

Clear, J. (n.d.). *How to start new habits that actually stick.* James Clear. https://jamesclear.com/three-steps-habit-change

Clear, J. (n.d.). *How to stop procrastinating by using the "2-minute rule."* James Clear. https://jamesclear.com/how-to-stop-procrastinating

Coaching Positive Performance. (n.d.). *The importance of motivation in tackling procrastination.* Coaching Positive Performance. www.coachingpositiveperformance.com/the-importance-of-motivation-in-tackling-procrastination/

Demers, J. (2014, December 3). *7 Procrastination excuses and how to defeat them.* Inc. www.inc.com/jayson-demers/7-procrastination-excuses-and-how-to-defeat-them.html

Grohol, J. M. (2019, May 15). *Learn about procrastination.* Psyche Central. https://psychcentral.com/lib/learn-about-procrastination/

James Cook University. (n.d.). *Procrastination and motivation.* James Cook University. www.jcu.edu.au/__data/assets/pdf_file/0004/392791/Information-Sheet-Procrastination-and-Motivation.pdf

Jane. (n.d.). *The procrastination cycle.* Habits for Wellbeing. www.habitsforwellbeing.com/the-procrastination-cycle/

Kamb, S. (2019, December 30). *5 Hacks to effortlessly build healthy habits in 2020.* Nerd Fitness. www.nerdfitness.com/blog/how-to-build-healthy-habits-that-stick/

Knaus, W. (2002, November 30). *The Procrastination Workbook.* http://library.deep-blue-sea.net/Procrastination/William%20Knaus-The%20procrastination%20workbook_%20your%20personalized%20program%20for%20breaking%20free%20from%20the%20patterns%20that%20hold%20you%20back-New%20Harbinger%20Publications%20(2002).pdf

Lazarus, C. N. (2010, August 7). *Beat procrastination: Do it now!* Psychology Today. www.psychologytoday.com/intl/blog/think-well/201008/beat-procrastination-do-it-now

Mind Tools Content Team. (n.d.). *Eisenhower's urgent/important principle.* Mind Tools. www.mindtools.com/pages/article/newHTE_91.htm

Mind Tools Content Team. (n.d.). *How to stop procrastinating.* Mind Tools. www.mindtools.com/pages/article/newHTE_96.htm

Newsonen, S. (2015, November 11). *6 Reasons why procrastination can be good for you.* Psychology Today. www.psychologytoday.com/intl/blog/the-path-passionate-happiness/201511/6-reasons-why-procrastination-can-be-good-you

Novotney, A. (2010, January). *Procrastination or 'intentional delay'?* American Psychological Association. www.apa.org/gradpsych/2010/01/procrastination

O'Donovan, K. (n.d.). *8 Dreadful effects of procrastination that can destroy your life.* Lifehack. www.lifehack.org/articles/productivity/8-ways-procrastination-can-destroy-your-life.html

Procrastination. (n.d.). http://www.basicknowledge101.com/pdf/Procrastination.pdf

Schraw, G., Wadkins, T., & Olafson, L. (2007). Doing the things we do: A grounded theory of academic procrastination. *Journal of Educational Psychology.* Vol. 99., Iss. 1., Pg. 12–25. https://psycnet.apa.org/record/2007-01726-002

Thome, A. (n.d.). *What is behavior-based goal setting? (And how can it help you get where you want?).* Girls Gone Strong. www.girlsgonestrong.com/blog/articles/what-is-behavior-based-goal-setting

Webb, D. (2016, January 20). *The five stages to successful behavior change.* Cecilia Health Marketing. www.ceceliahealth.com/blog/2016/1/20/the-five-stages-to-successful-behavior-change

Whitman College. (July 2015). *Motivation and procrastination.* Whitman College. www.whitman.edu/documents/Academics/Academic%20Support/Motivation%20and%20Procrastination.pdf

William, D. K. (2014, May 15). *10 Lame excuses you probably use to procrastinate.* The Web Writer Spotlight. https://webwriterspotlight.com/excuses-for-procrastinating

Winkowski, E. (2019, March 25). *Why you procrastinate (It has nothing to do with self-control).* The New York Times. www.nytimes.com/2019/03/25/smarter-living/why-you-procrastinate-it-has-nothing-to-do-with-self-control.html

www.ingramcontent.com/pod-product-compliance
Ingram Content Group UK Ltd.
Pitfield, Milton Keynes, MK11 3LW, UK
UKHW041956190726
13854UKWH00005B/2001

9 798674 897828